Just Plain Data Analysis

JUST PLAIN DATA ANALYSIS

Finding, Presenting, and Interpreting Social Science Data

SECOND EDITION

GARY M. KLASS

ROWMAN & LITTLEFIELD PUBLISHERS, INC.
Lanham • Boulder • New York • Toronto • Plymouth, UK

Published by Rowman & Littlefield Publishers, Inc.
A wholly owned subsidiary of The Rowman & Littlefield Publishing Group, Inc.
4501 Forbes Boulevard, Suite 200, Lanham, Maryland 20706
www.rowman.com

10 Thornbury Road, Plymouth PL6 7PP, United Kingdom

British Library Cataloguing in Publication Information Available

Library of Congress Cataloging-in-Publication Data

Klass, Gary M., 1952-
   Just plain data analysis : finding, presenting, and interpreting social science data /
Gary M. Klass. — 2nd ed.
      p. cm.
   ISBN 978-1-4422-1507-8 (cloth : alk. paper) — ISBN 978-1-4422-1508-5
   (pbk. : alk. paper) — ISBN 978-1-4422-1509-2 (electronic)
   1. Statistics. 2. Social sciences—Statistics. 3. Social sciences—Statistical methods.
   I. Title.
   HA29.K58 2012
   519.5—dc23   2012004619

♾️™ The paper used in this publication meets the minimum requirements of
American National Standard for Information Sciences—Permanence of Paper
for Printed Library Materials, ANSI/NISO Z39.48-1992.

Printed in the United States of America

To the thousands of Illinois State and
Illinois Wesleyan University students
who have spent their Saturday mornings
building eighteen Habitat for Humanity homes since 1995

Contents

Preface
What Is Just Plain Data Analysis?

66 JUST PLAIN data analysis" is, simply, the compilation and presentation of numerical evidence to support and illustrate arguments about politics and public affairs.

There is a realm of public debate about society's most contentious issues where arguments are grounded in hard evidence and sound reasoning. Often this evidence comes in the form of numerical measures of social conditions and of the effectiveness of public policies and governing institutions. When contending sides advance their causes by finding, presenting, and interpreting such evidence with clear thinking, the quality of public debate and the chances of devising effective solutions to society's problems are greatly increased.

The contending sides in such debate are rarely dispassionate and often present misleading evidence and deceptive reasoning, but the shortcomings of such arguments are transparent to those who can apply critical thinking skills to the evidence. This is often not the case in other realms of public debate, prevalent in today's broadcast media and, increasingly, in academic discourse, where competing anecdotes and malign characterizations of the other side's motives are all too common.

Just plain data analysis is the most common form of quantitative social science methodology, although the statistical literacy skills and knowledge it entails are often not presented, or presented well, in social science research methods and statistics textbooks. These skills involve finding, presenting, and interpreting numerical information in the form of commonly used social, political, and economic indicators. They are skills that students will find of considerable practical use, both in their subsequent coursework and in their future careers.

Just plain data analysis differs from what is commonly regarded as quantitative social science methodology in that it usually does not involve formal tests of theories, hypotheses, or null hypotheses. Rather than relying on statistical analysis of a single dataset, just plain data analysis, at its best, involves compiling all the relevant evidence from multiple data sources. Where conventional approaches to quantitative social science analysis stress the statistical analysis of data to model and test narrowly defined theories, just plain data analysis stresses presenting and critically evaluating statistical data to support arguments about social and political phenomena.

The best examples of just plain data analysis are found in many books that advance comprehensive and data-based arguments about social issues written by public intellectuals for a broad public audience. Often these works shape public debate about critical public policy issues. Charles Murray's 1984 book *Losing Ground*, for example, presented evidence of rising welfare caseloads and spending, undiminished poverty, and the breakdown of the two-parent family, which shaped conservative attacks on American welfare programs and eventually led to the dramatic welfare reform policies during the Clinton administration.[1] Employing much of the same method of analysis, Jeffrey Sachs's *The End of Poverty*, coming from a decidedly different ideological perspective, addresses issues of global poverty and may serve much the same role in spurring progressive solutions to the intractable poverty of third world nations.[2]

At times, both sides of a public debate use the same evidence to draw different conclusions. Thus, the annual *State of the World*[3] report published by the environmentalist organization Worldwatch Institute regularly describes the deterioration of the world's environment on a wide range of ecological indicators. Bjorn Lomborg's critique of that report in *The Skeptical Environmentalist*[4] counters with evidence that long-term trends in deforestation and in food, energy, and raw material production generally do not support the environmentalists' dire predictions.

In *The Politics of Rich and Poor*, historian Kevin Phillips argued that the Reagan administration policies were producing a new era of accelerating concentration of wealth, paralleling that of the Gilded Age and the Roaring Twenties. In tables and charts, Phillips presents statistic after statistic demonstrating that the United States has the highest inequalities of wealth and income in the developed world, the inequalities of wealth and income are steadily increasing, the divergence in pay between corporate executives and their employees is widening, and the rich are much richer and the poor and middle class poorer.[5] The theme, using the same Gilded Age metaphor and fifteen more years of evidence, is repeated with fewer tables and no charts, but often with a much more careful analysis of the statistical evidence in Paul Krugman's *The Conscience of a Liberal*.[6]

Robert Putnam's *Bowling Alone*, arguing that America faces a critical decline in social capital, is a classic example of just plain data analysis. Almost all of Putnam's analysis is grounded in quantitative data, from a wide variety of sources, presented in charts and graphs. Putnam describes his strategy as attempting to "triangulate among as many independent sources of information as possible" based on the "core principle" that "no single source of data is flawless, but the more numerous and diverse the sources, the less likely that they could all be influenced by the same flaw."[7] Legions of social scientists applied Putnam's core ideas to many fields of scholarly research, and public officials regularly cite his work in advancing new approaches to public issues.

No politician is as adept at the use of statistical evidence to support political arguments as is former president Bill Clinton. Clinton's most recent book is a broad critique of Republican anti–government policy agendas, an accounting of his own administration's success (and some of Obama's), and a detailed agenda for addressing current economic conditions.[8] Barely a page passes without the presentation of some numerical evidence, including many of the same statistical comparisons of the United States with other developed democracies contained in this book. His selection, presentation, and interpretation of the data are both self-congratulatory and partisan, but the effort challenges those who would disagree to counter with alternative data and explanations of their own.

Works such as these and others addressing public issues as diverse as gun control, the death penalty, racial and gender discrimination, national health care, school vouchers, and immigration advance the argument on one side of the public debate and often set the research agenda for additional social science research.

Students in almost every field of study encounter just plain data analysis all the time in the charts and tables presented in their textbooks and reading assignments. It is a primary mode of communication in government and is found in the studies, annual reports, and PowerPoint presentations of almost every governmental agency and advocacy group.

Just plain data analysis also plays an important role in the private sector, where compiling reliable and valid performance measures, effectively communicating numerical information to customers and employees, and evaluating data-based claims and conclusions are critical management talents. This, combined with having the confidence to base decisions on good data analysis even when tradition and conventional wisdom say otherwise, led to the remarkable achievements of the general manager of the Oakland Athletics, Billy Beane, depicted in Michael Lewis's book (and movie) *Moneyball*.[9]

Because Beane went straight from high school to a mediocre career playing professional baseball, he never had the opportunity to take a college statistics course. Yet Beane taught himself the science of sabermetrics, essentially the application of just plain data analysis to baseball statistics. As general manager of the Oakland Athletics, he used the statistics to identify undervalued trade and draft prospects (high school prospects were overvalued, walks were undervalued) and to make decisions traditionally left up to the team's manager (sacrifice bunts and intentional walks are often a bad idea). In his eleven years as general manager, Oakland achieved the fifth-best record in major league baseball despite having one of the lowest payrolls.

FINDING, PRESENTING, AND INTERPRETING THE DATA

There are three tasks and skills involved in doing just plain data analysis that traditional research methods courses and textbooks often neglect: finding, presenting, and interpreting numerical evidence.

Finding the Data

With the advances in information technology over the past decade, there has been a revolution in the amount and availability of statistical indicators provided by governments and nongovernmental public and private organizations. In addition to the volumes of data provided by the U.S. Census Bureau, many federal departments now have their own statistics agency, such as the National Center for Education Statistics, the Bureau of Justice Statistics, the National Center for Health Statistics, the Bureau of Labor Statistics, and the Bureau of Transportation Statistics, providing convenient online access to comprehensive data collections and statistical reports. In recent years, the greatest growth in the sheer quantity of statistical indicators has been in the field of education. The mandated testing under the No Child Left Behind Act and the expansion of the Department of Education's National Assessment of Educational Progress (*The Nation's Report Card*) have produced massive databases of measures of the performance of the nation's schools that, for better or worse, have fundamentally transformed the administration of educational institutions.

There has also been a significant growth in the quantity and quality of comparative international data. The Organisation for Economic Co-operation and Development (OECD) now provides a comprehensive range of governmental, social, and economic data for developed nations. For developing nations, the World Bank's development of poverty indicators and measures of business and economic conditions and the UN's Millennium Development Goals database have contributed greatly to public debate and analysis of national and international policies affecting impoverished people around the world. With the *Trends in International Mathematics and Science Study* (TIMSS) and the *Programme in International Student Assessment* (PISA) international educational achievement tests, rich databases of educational system conditions and student performance are now easily accessible.

A similar growth has taken place in the availability of social indicator data derived from nongovernmental public opinion surveys that offer consistent times series and cross-national measures of public attitudes and social behaviors. Time series indicators can be readily obtained online from the U.S. National Elections Study and the National Opinion Research Center's annual General Social Survey, and comparative cross-national data indicators can be accessed from Comparative Study of Electoral Systems, the International Social Survey Programme, and World Values Survey.

Finding the best data relevant to the analysis of contemporary social and political issues requires a basic familiarity with the kinds of data likely to be available from these sources. Social science research methods courses often give short shrift to this crucial stage of the research process, which involves skills and expertise usually acquired by years of experience in specific fields of study. Too often, the data are a given: the instructor gives a dataset to the students and asks them to analyze it. Finding the best data to address a research question requires that one understand the kinds of data that are likely to be available, who collects the data, and where they can be found.

Presenting the Data

Good data presentation skills are to data-based analysis what good writing is to literature, and some of the same basic principles apply to both. Poor graphical and tabular presentations often lead both readers and writers to draw erroneous conclusions from the data and obscure facts that better presentations would reveal. Some of these practices involve deliberate distortions of data, but more commonly they involve either unintentional distortions or simply ineffective approaches to presenting numerical evidence.

The past two decades have seen the development of a substantial literature on the art and science of data presentation, much of it following Edward R. Tufte's path-breaking work *The Visual Display of Quantitative Information*.[10] With his admonitions to "show the data," "minimize the ink-to-data ratio," and avoid "ChartJunk," Tufte established many of the basic rules and principles of data presentation and demonstrated over and over again how effective data presentations combined with clear thinking can reveal truths hidden in the data. Howard Wainer's work extended Tufte's standards, with a somewhat greater focus on tabular displays of data.[11]

Few if any research methods and statistics texts address these standards of data presentation in more than a cursory manner, and many demonstrate some of the worst data presentation practices. Although the development of spreadsheet and other software has greatly simplified the tasks of tabular and graphical data presentation, it has also greatly facilitated some very bad data presentation practices.

Interpreting the Data

Good data analysis entails little more than finding the best data relevant to a given research question, making meaningful comparisons among the data, and drawing sound conclusions from the comparisons. To evaluate arguments based on numerical evidence, one must first assess the reliability and validity of the individual measures used and then evaluate the validity of causal conclusions drawn from comparisons of the data.

Assessing the reliability and validity of social indicator measurements requires that one understand how the data are collected and how the indicators are constructed. Many research methods and statistics texts address issues of measurement merely as matters of choosing the appropriate level of measurement for variables (nominal, ordinal, and interval) and of calculating sampling error. As a practical matter, such issues are usually irrelevant or trivial when one undertakes to do just plain data analysis. With just plain data analysis, almost all of the data are interval measures in the form of ratios, percentages, and means, even if the base question for the indicator is nominal or ordinal.

Although they are often the only measurement reliability issue addressed in statistics courses, measures of sampling error usually constitute the least important aspect of measurement reliability. In chapter 1, we will see that the least reliable measures of crime rates, based on the FBI Uniform Crime Reports, have far less sampling error (actually no sampling error) than the more reliable measures based on the National Crime Victimization Surveys. The same thing occurs with the measurement of educational achievement discussed in chapter 8: the No Child Left Behind tests of all students are shown to be less reliable that the National Assessment of Education Progress tests based on national samples of students.

Implicitly or explicitly, almost all meaningful data analysis serves the purpose of supporting conclusions related to causation. When people are presented with numerical information that runs counter to their previously held beliefs, we often hear the statement "You can prove anything with statistics." This is true, except that it usually takes something more than just the statistics: faulty logic and reasoning. Chapter 3—the most crucial chapter in this book—presents a series of errors of logic in the form of statistical fallacies, paradoxes, and threats to validity that often lead people to draw faulty conclusions from numerical comparisons. These fallacies serve as a framework for analyzing empirical evidence of causal relationships and identifying additional numerical comparisons to resolve competing explanations.

Why We Should Teach Just Plain Data Analysis

Often, a fear of mathematics combined with nonsequential curricular requirements leads students to take a research methods and statistics course only in their last semester of study. In departments that require freshmen to take introductory methods courses, the required course is often the last time in students' academic careers that they will actually do the quantitative analysis that is taught. It may even be the last time they will have to read research employing the methods that are taught.

Just plain data analysis involves skills and expertise that students can readily apply to the analysis of evidence presented in their course literature, in conducting their own research for term papers, and in independent study projects. In addition, the data analysis and data presentation skills described here have widespread application in a wide range of future careers in both government and the private sector. It is not too late to read this text in the last semester of your senior year of college, but it is later than it should have been.

Those students who will go on to learn and apply the knowledge of the central limit theorem, multiple regression, factor analysis, and other less-plain statistical applications will discover that many of the principles of just plain data analysis will greatly improve the quality of their work.

Most importantly, in today's world the exercise of effective citizenship increasingly requires a public competent to evaluate positions grounded in numerical arguments. As the role of government has expanded to affect almost every aspect of people's daily lives, the role of statistics in shaping governmental policies has expanded as well. To the extent the public lacks the skills to critically evaluate the statistical analyses that shape public policy, more and more crucial decisions that affect our daily lives will be made by technocrats who have these skills or by others who would use their mastery of these skills to serve their own partisan or special-interest ends.

In collecting and presenting the data in this book, I have tried to be evenhanded, nonpartisan, and to avoid imposing my own (inconsistent and often changing) political beliefs. Even a cursory reading of the text, however, will suggest that there is a persistent pattern to some of the data presented here.

There are tables and charts throughout this book in which the United States is compared to other nations on a variety of social indicators and measures of policy performance. The data show that, in comparison to other wealthy nations, the United States has by far the highest level of health care spending combined with the lowest life expectancy and highest infant mortality rate, the highest levels of income inequality and child poverty, the highest rate (in the whole world) of incarcerating its population, mediocre scores on international tests of educational achievement, the highest rate of spending on higher education combined with college graduation rates that are rapidly being surpassed by other nations, and among the lowest rates of voter turnout. If there had been room, I might have added data showing the United States with the highest maternal mortality rates, the highest teen pregnancy rates, the highest murder rates, almost the lowest level of taxation, and defense spending almost equal to the rest of the world's combined. I can't find the data, but I suspect that Americans spend several times more on election campaigns than the rest of the world combined. On several of these indicators, the United States ranks not only as worst among wealthy nations but on par with many developing nations.

All this gives a different meaning to the concept of "American exceptionalism"—a phrase most commonly used in the sentence, "Obama doesn't believe in American exceptionalism." I offer these numbers as a challenge to engage citizens who might be moved to ask these data two questions: "Why?" and "Why not?"

ORGANIZATION OF THIS BOOK

Chapter 1 begins with a discussion of the construction and practical uses of social indicator data and the analysis of the reliability and validity of the measures. The purpose is to give students a broad overview of the kind of data that are available, the many choices involved in the construction of social indicators, and the considerations involved in evaluating the use of specific indicators. Chapter 2, addressing the measurement of racial and ethnic inequality, is intended to provide examples of the variety of indicators that are available and that can be used to measure conditions associated with income and wealth, health care, education, and crime and punishment.

Chapter 3, containing a series of statistical fallacies, paradoxes, and threats to validity, is the most significant addition to the second edition of this book. Statistical fallacies (and the paradoxes and threats to validity) are common misinterpretations of statistical evidence that occur when the numerical evidence cited in an argument is not sufficient to support the conclusion.

Chapters 3 and 4 are modeled after each of two classic articles by Donald T. Campbell and H. Laurence Ross on "quasi-experiments": one on the Connecticut crackdown on speeding and the other on the British Breathalyzer experiment.[12] Campbell and Ross begin by listing and describing a series of threats to external validity that might account for a possibly spurious relationship between a policy change and a measure of a policy outcome. They then apply the framework to test the hypotheses that the two policy changes resulted in improved traffic safety. Chapter 4 applies the framework of fallacies, paradoxes, and Campbell and Ross's threats to validity to an analysis of the effect of the Rudy Giuliani mayoralty on New York City crime rates.

Chapters 5 and 6 illustrate many of the basic principles of the art and science of data presentation in tables and charts and contain several examples of bad tabular and graphic design.

Chapters 7, 8, and 9 apply and illustrate the principles of the earlier chapters in more detail, focusing on the topics of voting, education, and poverty. Each of these chapters begins with a discussion of comparative international statistical measures, followed by U.S. data, and ends with evaluations of specific examples of data-based arguments.

A companion website for this text (http://pol.illinoisstate.edu/jpda/) contains hyperlinks to all the spreadsheet files used to construct the tables and charts, complete citations for the original data sources, and links to the data sources.

All of the charts prepared for this book were constructed with the 2011 version of Microsoft Excel charting software. Some charting functions shown on the charts, particularly the boxplots and the data labels shown on the scatterplots, did require the use of free downloadable add-ins. The companion website contains links to those add-ins and instructions, tips, and tricks for using Excel to do the things demonstrated in the book.

NOTES

1. Charles Murray, *Losing Ground: American Social Policy, 1950–1980* (New York: Basic Books, 1984); see also Murray, *Coming Apart: The State of White America, 1960-2010* (New York: Crown Forum, 2012).

2. Jeffrey Sachs, *The End of Poverty: Economic Possibilities for Our Time* (New York: Penguin, 2005); see also Sachs, *The Price of Civilization: Reawakening American Virtue and Prosperity* (New York: Random House, 2011).

3. Worldwatch Institute, *The State of the World, 2006* (New York: Norton, 2006).

4. Bjorn Lomborg, *The Skeptical Environmentalist* (Cambridge, UK: Cambridge University Press, 2001).

5. Kevin Phillips, *The Politics of Rich and Poor: Wealth and the American Electorate in the Reagan Aftermath* (New York: HarperPerrenial, 1991).

6. Paul Krugman, *The Conscience of a Liberal* (New York: Norton, 2007).

7. Robert D. Putnam, *Bowling Alone* (New York: Simon & Schuster, 2000), 419.

8. Bill Clinton, *Back to Work: Why We Need Smart Government for a Strong Economy* (New York: Knopf, 2011).

9. Michael Lewis, *Moneyball: The Art of Winning an Unfair Game* (New York: Norton, 2004).

10. Edward Tufte, *The Visual Display of Quantitative Information* (Cheshire, CT: Graphics Press, 1993).

11. Howard Wainer, *Visual Revelations: Graphical Tales of Fate and Deception from Napoleon Bonaparte to Ross Perot* (Mahwah, NJ: Lawrence Erlbaum, 1997).

12. Donald T. Campbell and H. Laurence Ross, "The Connecticut Crackdown on Speeding: Time-Series Data in Quasi-Experimental Analysis," *Law & Society Review* 3, no. 1 (1968): 33–53; H. Laurence Ross, Donald T. Campbell, and Gene V. Glass, "Determining the Social Effects of a Legal Reform: The British 'Breathalyser' Crackdown of 1967," *American Behavioral Scientist* 13, no. 4 (March 1970): 493–509.

Acknowledgments

T HE STARTING point for this book was a research methods course I taught to political science students at Binghamton University at a time when analyzing data required the use of keypunch and punch-card-sorter machines. I have taught the "methods" course many times since, each time adding more and more of the practical data analysis material presented in this book. From the students in these courses, I have learned what they find most perplexing and challenging about data analysis, and they have challenged me to find better ways of presenting this material.

Working on their "data profile" term papers, many students discovered datasets and data sources that I was not familiar with and that are cited throughout this book. Three students in my quantitative reasoning course contributed more directly: Lesley Clements, Molly Miles, and Shannon Durocher offered excellent suggestions and identified some crucial errors.

To prepare the tables and charts in this book, I acquired a near mastery of the 2003 Microsoft Excel spreadsheet software and a considerable experience with the 2010 version. Excel is much more powerful than the card-sorter, but the frustrations are the same. My masters in my quest to earn a black belt in Excel charting were the regular contributors to the microsoft.public.excel.charting newsgroup: Rob Bovey, Debra Dalgleish, Tushar Mehta, Jon Peltier, Andy Pope, and John Walkenbach. Over and over again they found solutions to what, for me, were the most unsolvable charting problems. Their replies to my inquiries—and those of thousands of novice and experienced charters—were often simple, direct, and quick, and always courteous.

I am deeply indebted to my colleagues for their encouragement and comments on the convention papers that led to this book, the first edition, and on the initial drafts of the manuscript: Ky Ajayi, Jack Chizmar, Gary King, Milo Shield, Howard Wainer, Bill Wilkerson, and (much more than a colleague) Patricia Klass. For their proofreading and editing of the manuscript I am indebted for the excellent contributions of two Illinois State graduate students, Jennifer Swanson and Kara Bavery, and to Illinois State's greatest manuscript editor, Pat McCarney.

And finally, for their professionalism, encouragement, and assistance, many thanks to Niels Aaboe, Asa Johnson, Jon Sisk, Lynn Weber, and Darcy Evans at Rowman & Littlefield.

CHAPTER 1

Measuring Political, Social, and Economic Conditions

> I believe that the healthcare bill that was enacted by the current Congress will kill jobs in America, ruin the best healthcare system in the world, and bankrupt our country.
>
> —JOHN BOEHNER[1]

THROUGHOUT the 2010 Congressional election campaign, at town hall meetings, Tea Party rallies, and Congressional hearings, and on cable news talk shows, Americans debated the merits of legislation that the opponents argued would lead to a government takeover of "the best healthcare system in the world" and that supporters insisted would reform "the most expensive and least effective" of the world's health care systems.

Each side offered what it thought were telling statistics to support its case.[2] On the liberal side, those in favor of the Democratic bills being debated in Congress argued that the American health care system produced some of the worst health outcomes in the developing world. In comparison to other developed democracies (table 1.1), the United States was spending about twice as much per capita for its health care, 50 percent more than the next-highest nation. Infant (and maternal) mortality rates exceeded those of all other developed nations, while Americans' life expectancy was shorter than that of any developed, and many developing, nations. Among all the nations in the world, forty-three had lower infant mortality rates than the United States, and forty-nine had a higher life expectancy.[3] Forty-five million Americans, 16 percent of the population, lacked health insurance, most of them living in households where someone worked at a full-time job. Health care premiums were "skyrocketing," creating a vicious spiral of rising costs and fewer employees covered by insurance.

The anti-"Obamacare" side challenged the validity of some of these numbers and the relevance of the others. The infant mortality numbers are

TABLE 1.1
Health Care Indicators

	United States	21 Wealthy Democracies*			US Rank (/22)
		Lowest	Average	Highest	
Health Expenditures, 2008					
% of GDP	16.0	6.8	9.4	11.2	1
% private	53.5	15.5	23.7	40.9	1
per capita, US $:					
-total	$7,538	2,151	3,543	5,003	1
-public	$3,507	1,539	2,687	4,213	3(/20)
-pharmaceuticals	$876	251	475	665	1
Health conditions: 2007					
obesity rate, age 15+	34.1	3.4	14.3	26.5	1
% daily smokers	16.7	14.5	22.5	31.0	20
Health outcomes, 2007					
life expectancy (years):					
-at birth	77.9	78.4	80.4	82.6	22
-- females at age 65	19.7	19.2	21.0	23.6	21
-- males at age 66	17.1	16.5	17.7	18.6	17
infant mortality rate**	6.4	1.8	3.6	5.1	1
cancer deaths per 100,000 pop.	158	136	160	199	9(/17)
5-year survival rates:					
-prostate cancer	91.9	41.5	65.1	83.6	1(/16)
-breast cancer	83.9	71.9	77.7	82.6	1(/16)
Health resources, 2007					
MRI units per 1 mill. pop.	25.9	5.1	13.6	43.1	2(/16)
physicians, per 1,000 pop.	2.4	2.2	3.3	4.5	13(/15)

*Australia, Austria, Belgium, Canada, Denmark, Finland, France, Germany, Iceland, Ireland, Italy, Japan, Luxembourg, Netherlands, New Zealand, Norway, Portugal, Spain, Sweden, Switzerland, United Kingdom
** per 1,000 live births
Source: OECD Health Data 2010

suspect, they said, because of differences in how some countries count live births. The life expectancy and infant mortality have more to do with lifestyle choices than with the quality of the health care system: Americans have the highest rates of obesity in the world and world-leading murder and accident rates.[4] Almost 9 million of the 45 million said to lack health insurance were not even American citizens. Many others could afford private insurance but had not chosen to purchase it, or they were eligible for Medicaid but had not sought coverage. The anti-Obamacare side cited data indicating that the United States leads the world in cancer and preterm-baby survival rates and that Americans enjoy greater access to the most advanced medical technology and treatments. Waiting times for necessary medical treatments, they insisted, were much longer in countries such as England and Canada that had government-run health care or health insurance.

All of this evidence, and much more, was presented to the American people, scrutinized and critiqued in books, reports, editorials, letters to the editor, research papers, and blogs. Some people respond to arguments such as these with glazed eyes and say, "You can prove anything with statistics," and some of them go on to say, "Besides, it's all just a matter of opinion." In my opinion, those people are wrong.

What we have here is a debate involving not just two different opinions, but two conflicting arguments drawing nearly opposite conclusions from numerical evidence. One of these arguments is stronger than the other; it is supported by better evidence and sounder reasoning. The other argument is weaker; it relies more on irrelevant and misleading evidence and fallacious reasoning. I know which is the better argument, but I'm not going to tell you. Better, I think, that you learn how to analyze the statistical indicators, to be aware of the strengths and weaknesses in the evidence each side offers.

The numbers in table 1.1 are just a sample of the many measures of the performance of the American health care system. Many more social, economic, and political indicators measure the performance of other institutions and sectors of the economy affecting every aspect of American life: energy production and consumption, the environment, agriculture, transportation, education, voting and elections, crime and law enforcement, and business and labor markets. The indicators are standardized numerical measurements of the performance of societies' institutions, the evidence that grounds public debate over matters of social policy and public affairs, and the tools of social science research directed to identifying solutions to society's most pressing problems. Most crucially, numerical indicators are the standards by which citizens measure the performance of their elected officials and governmental agencies and hold them accountable for their work.

While Congress debated the health care legislation, the United States became enmeshed in its deepest economic recession since the Great Depression. The causes and probable duration of the current Great Recession are still a matter of much debate, but the data in figure 1.1 provide some insight into the nature of the crisis. Some say the problems started with what now looks like a relatively mild economic downturn that followed the attacks on 9/11. In response, the Federal Reserve eased monetary policy, resulting in lower mortgage interest rates and higher home prices. The housing price bubble was fueled by worldwide investment in several profitable new American inventions: highly leveraged mortgage-backed securities, liar loans, subprime mortgages, and credit default swaps. Mortgage rates started to rise in 2004 and 2005, and when homeowners discovered in late 2007 that they could not refinance their subprime and adjustable-rate mortgages, the bubble burst. The banking sector collapsed; gas prices peaked, then fell; and the stock market crashed in 2008.

As unemployment and poverty rates increased, the Bush and Obama administrations and the Federal Reserve responded with unprecedented stimulus measures. By 2010, the stock market had made up some of the loss, but unemployment remained high and home prices continued to fall. The Bush administration bailouts of the banking industry and the Obama administration economic stimulus have left the federal government facing huge budget deficits, with the national debt forecast to double every eight years.

THE USE OF SOCIAL INDICATORS

For partisan and nonpartisan policy analysts who seek to identify solutions to the nation's most pressing problems, social indicators provide answers to the questions they address: Do firearms laws, or the death penalty, reduce murder rates? Would public school students perform better in private schools? Do tax cuts spur economic growth? Do they favor the rich? Do motorcycle helmet and seat belt laws reduce traffic fatalities? Are racial and gender disparities in income and poverty a consequence of societal discrimination? Does national health insurance result in better health care?

It is true, as we will see, that the answers to these questions are seldom clear-cut, and the "statistics" are often used to deceive and mislead. But analysis and argument grounded in a thoughtful analysis of statistical evidence have many advantages over the increasingly common alternative: arguments grounded in ideological presupposition and aspersions of motive. Statistical deceptions are often transparent; those who understand how the statistics are calculated, the limitations of the data, and the

Figure 1.1. Political and Economic Indicators, 2000–2011.

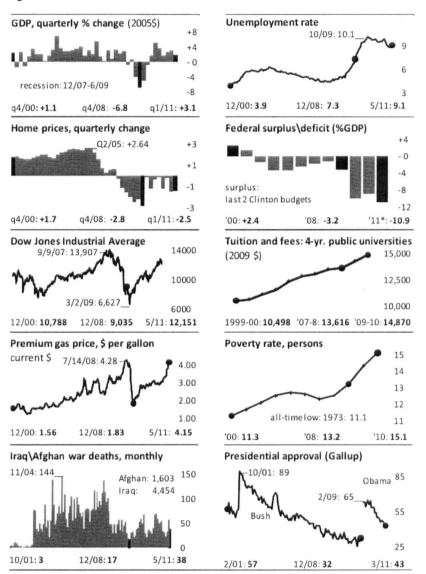

GDP, quarterly % change (2005$)

recession: 12/07-6/09

+8
+4
- 0
-4
-8

q4/00: **+1.1**   q4/08: **-6.8**   q1/11: **+3.1**

Unemployment rate

10/09: 10.1

9
6
3

12/00: **3.9**   12/08: **7.3**   5/11: **9.1**

Home prices, quarterly change

Q2/05: +2.64

+3
+1
-1
-3

q4/00: **+1.7**   q4/08: **-2.8**   q1/11: **-2.5**

Federal surplus\deficit (%GDP)

surplus:
last 2 Clinton budgets

+4
- 0
-4
-8
-12

'00: **+2.4**   '08: **-3.2**   '11*: **-10.9**

Dow Jones Industrial Average

9/9/07: 13,907

3/2/09: 6,627

14000
10000
6000

12/00: **10,788**   12/08: **9,035**   5/11: **12,151**

Tuition and fees: 4-yr. public universities
(2009 $)

15,000
12,500
10,000

1999-00: **10,498**   '07-8: **13,616**   '09-10: **14,870**

Premium gas price, $ per gallon

current $ 7/14/08: 4.28

4.00
3.00
2.00
1.00

12/00: **1.56**   12/08: **1.83**   5/11: **4.15**

Poverty rate, persons

all-time low: 1973: 11.1

15
14
13
12
11

'00: **11.3**   '08: **13.2**   '10: **15.1**

Iraq\Afghan war deaths, monthly

11/04: 144

Afghan: 1,603
Iraq: 4,454

150
100
50
0

10/01: **3**   12/08: **17**   5/11: **38**

Presidential approval (Gallup)

-10/01: 89

Obama

2/09: 65

Bush

85
55
25

2/01: **57**   12/08: **32**   3/11: **43**

Sources: Bureau of Economic Analysis, Bureau of Labor Statistics, Federal Housing Finance Agency, Office of Management and Budget, Yahoo! Finance, National Center for Education Statistics, Energy Information Administration, Census Bureau, Icasualties.org, Gallup (see companion website).

limitations of the methods of analysis will not be easily fooled. It is a lot easier to show that an interpretation of a statistic is false than it is to disprove allegations that people or groups take particular policy positions because "liberals hate America" or "conservatives hate the poor."

The power of political arguments grounded in statistical evidence was illustrated by a rejoinder Senator Daniel Patrick Moynihan (D-NY) often used in political debates: "You are entitled to your own opinion," he would say, "but you are not entitled to your own facts."[5]

WHERE THE NUMBERS COME FROM

Those who originally prepared and reported these statistics did so without any assurance as to just how the numbers might be used, but they understand that responsible statistical reporting can have unanticipated beneficial consequences. In 2006, financier Warren Buffett pledged most of his $40 billion wealth to the Bill and Melinda Gates Foundation to support the organization's efforts to address health care needs in developing nations. The Gates Foundation was established after Buffett asked Bill Gates to read the disheartening news in the World Bank's *1993 World Development Report*, a detailed statistical summary of economic and health care conditions in the world's poorest nations.[6]

Although collecting and reporting columns of numbers can be tedious and dispassionate work, the task is not without political ramifications. During the Nixon administration, Ruth Leger Sivard served as chief economist for the U.S. State Department's Arms Control and Disarmament Agency with responsibility for the agency's annual report, *World Military Expenditures*, the most authoritative source of data on military, health, and education spending in countries across the world.[7] In 1972, the secretary of defense complained to the president that the nonmilitary data in the report embarrassed allies and undermined congressional support for the defense budget. Soon the State Department decided to stop reporting the education and health data.[8] In response, Sivard resigned her government position, set up her own private nonprofit educational publishing company, and with the help of student volunteers, began publishing her own annual report, *World Military and Social Expenditures*, in competition with the government.[9] More than the original ACDA report, the new report highlighted the guns and butter trade-offs and the disparities in wealth between the world's rich and poor nations. For her efforts, Sivard received the UNESCO Prize for Peace Education in 1991.

Just about every aspect of the daily lives of Americans is the subject of data collection by some governmental statistical agency. The Bureau of Labor Statistics reports monthly data on employment, wages, and salaries in almost every sector of the economy and measures how much consumers pay for almost everything they purchase. The National Agricultural Statistics Service's data cover every aspect of the farm economy: who owns and works on the farms; how much of each crop is planted, harvested, and exported; and farm prices and earnings. The National Center for Educational Statistics measures graduation rates; student performance on math, science, reading, and history tests; how much is spent for schooling; how much time students spend in class, doing homework, reading, watching TV, working on computers, and exercising; and how much the teachers get paid. The National Center for Health Statistics provides data on almost everything related to health care conditions and services: diseases, birthrates and death rates, obesity rates, condom use, and statistics on hospitals, physicians, and nurses. The Department of Transportation's National Center for Statistics and Analysis records the circumstances of every traffic fatality. The Energy Information Administration provides data on energy production, consumption, and prices. Crime rates are reported by both the FBI and the Bureau of Justice Statistics. Other statistical agencies—often agencies within the same departments—provide data on a wide range of other topics, ranging from air pollution, global temperature and carbon dioxide levels, to housing prices.

By far the largest statistical agency, however, is the U.S. Census Bureau, and its statistics are based only in part on the decennial Census. The decennial Census of Population and Housing provides a more or less accurate count of the entire U.S. population, with demographic data that are reported down to the level of city blocks. But the Census also conducts surveys of samples of American households, among them the monthly Current Population Survey and the annual American Community Survey, as well as two five-year censuses of governments and the economy.

CONSTRUCTING SOCIAL INDICATORS: COUNT, DIVIDE, AND COMPARE

Analyzing and interpreting social indicators requires a competent understanding of where the data come from, how the data are collected, and how the indicators are constructed. In general, three components are involved in the use of any social indicator: the counts, the divisors, and the comparisons.[10]

The Counts

The defining element of a social indicator is the statistic's numerator: the count. Most social indicator counts are based on enumerations derived from either survey questions or agency records. In the case of U.S. infant mortality rate statistics, for example, the counts of infant deaths are obtained from tallies of local death certificates (the divisors are obtained from enumerations of birth certificates). The Bureau of Labor Statistics counts as unemployed anyone who does not have a full-time or part-time job and is actively looking for work. The counts of the unemployed are derived from surveys involving several questions concerning the respondent's employment status. Some measures of voter turnout are based on counts of the number of voters who show up at the polls; others on the number of votes cast; still others on estimates derived from postelection surveys—counts of respondents who claim they have voted. Poverty rates may be based on counts of the number of persons living in poor families or counts of the number of poor families. The Federal Bureau of Investigation's crime rate statistics are based on counts of specific crimes reported to local police departments. The Bureau of Justice Statistics calculates a different crime rate statistic using counts of respondents' reports of crimes in household surveys.

Interpreting the social indicators and avoiding misinterpretations requires a good understanding of the actual survey questions and definitions and standards used to determine the counts. What seems to be a straightforward statistic is often the product of a quite complex process. To count the number of families living in poverty, for example, the Census Bureau first has to determine the levels of income below which different size families will be considered poor. Then it must determine what constitutes a family's income (food stamps and earned income tax benefits are not counted; welfare and social security payments are). Think that is easy? Now imagine what goes into defining exactly what is and is not a family.

The Divisors

Most social indicators consist of both a numerator (the count) and a denominator (the divisor). For any given social indicator count—such as the health care expenditures shown in table 1.1—a variety of social indicators can be constructed using different denominators. Measuring health care expenditures as a percentage of gross domestic product is a standard method of adjusting the data for differences in the size of national economies. National health care expenditures can also be reported per capita (to adjust for the size of the countries' populations), in U.S. dollars (to adjust for differences in currency), and weighted by OECD's purchasing power parity index (PPP) (to adjust for differences in prices across countries).

For any given population count, there are often several choices of divisors that can be used to construct an indicator. Consider, for example, the many ways one could go about measuring the divorce rate:

- The number of divorces in a year divided by the number of marriages (this is referred to as the divorce ratio).
- The number of divorces divided by the number of married couples.
- The number of divorced persons divided by the number of married persons.
- The percentage of couples who stay married beyond their fifth, tenth, and succeeding anniversaries.
- The number of divorces divided by the population.

The last of these, a very unsatisfactory measure, is the official divorce rate.

Common divisors used in the construction of social indicators are population (e.g., murders per 100,000 population), gross domestic product (military expenditures as a percentage of GDP), and median family income (university tuition and fees as a percentage of median family income). Other indicators use divisors tailored for specific counts. Highway fatality rates are often measured per 100 million vehicle miles traveled, but also per 100,000 licensed drivers, per 100,000 vehicles registered, and per 100,000 population. Abortion *rates* measure the number of abortions per 1,000 women aged 15 to 44. Abortion *ratios* measure the number of abortions per 1,000 live births.

Careful attention to the divisor is often crucial to statistical analysis. It is possible for the abortion rate to increase at the same time the abortion ratio is in decline. Sparsely populated states usually have very low traffic fatality rates measured in terms of miles traveled, but high fatality rates when population is the divisor. Military expenditures as a percentage of GDP may go into decline only because the economy is rapidly growing.

When comparing changes over time in monetary measures, such as per capita income or college tuition, it is often best to report the data in constant rather than current dollars. Constant dollars are current dollars adjusted for inflation. This is most commonly done by dividing the current dollars by the consumer price index, the Bureau of Labor Statistics measure of inflation.

The Comparisons

The purpose of any measurement is to make a comparison. Most analyses of social indicators involve one or a combination of three forms of numerical comparison: cross-sectional comparisons, cross-time comparisons, and comparisons across demographic categories.

The health expenditure data shown in table 1.1 involve cross-sectional (specifically, cross-national) comparisons. Cross-sectional comparisons often involve comparing performance measures across nations, states, cities, or institutions, often to determine whether a particular jurisdiction is doing better or worse than the standards achieved by others. Thus, as we will see in chapter 8, a national task-force report on the condition of American education, *A Nation at Risk*, began by describing the relatively poor performance of American students on international mathematics and science tests.[11] Studies of the American death penalty or gun control laws often begin by citing the statistical evidence that the United States has the highest murder rate of any developed nation. Studies of American health policy begin by noting that among developed nations, the United States has the highest infant mortality rate, relatively low life expectancy, the highest level of health care expenditure, and the lowest rates of health insurance coverage. Other studies note the relatively high rates of energy consumption, incarceration, child poverty, inequality, and teenage pregnancy in the United States, conditions ameliorated, perhaps, by our high GDP and low income taxes.

Often the best source of data for U.S. comparisons is the Organisation for Economic Co-operation and Development (OECD), an international organization of thirty-four high-income democracies based in Paris. The OECD compiles economic, governmental, and social data from member countries; establishes standards for consistent data definitions; and produces research reports and forecasts on a variety of topics.

Time series comparisons of social indicators are often the crucial evidence employed in arguments about politics and public policy. In contemporary political debate, trends in social policy indicators are most often cited to implicitly or explicitly assign blame to some governmental agency or official, but on occasion they are employed solely to issue public warning of impending adversity. Such is the case with the most portentous time series comparison of our time: the global temperature data, shown in figure 1.2.

Although for a time this evidence of global warming (represented by the hockey stick shape of the post-1940 trend, first described in the work of Michael E. Mann, Raymond S. Bradley, and Malcolm K. Hughes)[12] was hotly contested, few now question the validity of these data. The policy debates have not ended, however, and additional data and comparisons are now the evidence for debate over forecasts of continued temperature increases, explanations of the causes of the global warming, and evaluations of policy changes that might address the problem.

Figure 1.2. Global Land-Ocean Surface Temperature Anomalies (annual mean, in degrees Celsius).

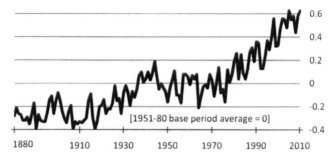

Source: Goddard Institute for Space Studies.

A great deal of social science research is premised on evidence involving comparisons across *demographic categories*, such as those defined by age, race, nationality, religion, education, and income level. In the chapters that follow, we will see evidence of demographic disparities in social indicators that have profound and puzzling implications for society and politics: The elderly are more likely to vote than the young. The elderly are much less likely to be poor than are children. Women earn less than men. The rich are getting richer and the poor, poorer. Frequent churchgoers are more likely to vote than non-churchgoers, or, maybe, lie about whether they have voted.

Combining time series comparisons with cross-sectional or demographic comparisons often provides for a richly detailed analysis. For example, policy analysts often use the word "skyrocketing" to describe the steadily increasing share of the U.S. GDP allocated to health care costs, far outpacing the rate of growth in any other developed nation (figure 1.3).

Figure 1.3. Health Expenditures, % of GDP, 22 Wealthy OECD Nations, 1960–2008.

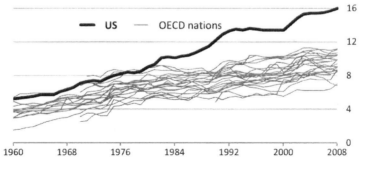

Source: OECD Health Data 2010.

Figure 1.4. Life Expectancy, 22 Wealthy OECD Nations, 1960–2008.

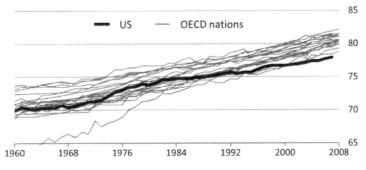

Source: OECD Health Data 2010.

Time series comparisons are used to evaluate the effects of specific policy changes. The Medicare system, created in 1965, did much to increase demand for medical services but never included any effective cost control measures. The most transformative legislation designed to control health care costs, the 1973 Health Maintenance Organization Act, does not seem to have brought about the anticipated decline in health care costs. Notice how U.S. health expenditures seem to stabilize in the 1990s? Mostly this had to do with rising GDP during the Clinton administration. Health care costs were still going up, but the rest of the economy was growing just as fast.

We can then take these comparisons a step further by comparing indicators. A comparison of the health expenditure data in figure 1.3 with the life expectancy data in figure 1.4 clearly suggests that increased health care spending has not produced commensurate health outcomes.

MEASUREMENT VALIDITY AND RELIABILITY

To evaluate arguments based on social indicators, it is first necessary to determine whether the statistics are trustworthy. Two standards guide the choice and interpretation of a social indicator: measurement validity and measurement reliability. An indicator is *valid* to the degree that it actually measures the general concept or phenomenon under consideration. An indicator is *reliable* to the degree that the measurement is consistent and unbiased.

Measurement Validity

To evaluate the validity of a social indicator, one must consider the context in which it is used and the choices made in determining the indicator's counts and divisors.

Conservatives who argued that infant mortality and life expectancy are not good measures of the quality of the U.S. health care system were questioning the validity of the data. Many people question the validity of SAT scores, arguing that the tests do not measure what they are intended to measure, or that they measure only a narrow range of intellectual abilities, such as test-taking ability.[13] Whether an indicator is valid depends on the context and purposes for which it is used. Some insist that the validity of the SAT is confirmed by how well it predicts students' future college performance, but this begs the question of just what it is that is doing the predicting. Because only those students who intend to go on to college take the SAT, the scores are probably not a valid indicator of the quality of the instruction in individual high schools or courses. Nevertheless, the often-reported average SAT scores of college and university freshman classes is probably the best indicator of the selectivity of schools' admission standards.

Often the general concept of interest is ambiguous, or for other reasons, there is no direct measure of the concept at issue. To address this, researchers may combine a variety of different measures of the underlying concept. In *Bowling Alone*, Robert Putnam employs several different indicators to measure the concept of "social capital," or the quality of human interactions contributing to civic purposes. Putnam's indicators included trends in television viewing, charitable giving, church attendance, volunteerism rates, suicide rates, statewide ballot initiatives, giving the finger to other drivers, and (what gives the book its title) participation in league bowling. To measure the level of social capital across the fifty states, Putnam developed a single *Social Capital Index*, a weighted average of fourteen measures of community life, engagement in public affairs (e.g., voter turnout), volunteerism, and survey responses to questions regarding social trust and sociability.[14]

In 2000, the World Health Organization's annual *World Health Report* included a ranking-based index for the critical features of the health care delivery system of 190 countries, ranking each country on eight indicators related to overall spending, the fairness of the health care finance system, the overall health of its population, and mortality amenable to health care.[15] The United States ranked 37 on the combined indicator.

Similar indexes are used in a wide variety of areas in social science research. In the 1970s, the Overseas Development Council developed a Physical Quality of Life Index (PQLI), a combination of life expectancy, infant mortality, and literacy rates as an alternative to the use of gross national product as a measure of a country's well-being.[16] Later, economist Mahbub ul Haq developed the UN's Human Development Index, based on per capita GDP, life expectancy, and education.

Measurement Reliability

If students who took the SAT several times were likely to get wildly differ-ent scores each time (assuming their intellectual ability had remained the same), the test would be unreliable. Unreliability can be caused by errors in data collection, changes in survey procedures, and occasionally, changes in what people mean by their responses to the same question asked at different times. Even the best data collection efforts are subject to errors that affect data reliability. After several decades of Census undercounts, the Census Bureau's final analysis of the 2000 Census indicated that it had overcounted the nation's population by 1.3 million persons: 5.8 million persons were duplicate counts; 4.5 million were not counted at all.[17]

Cross-national data are particularly subject to inconsistent collection and reporting. Although the World Bank, the United Nations, and the OECD strive to maintain consistent definitions and standards of measurement for the indicators they collect, they rely on national governments and other international organizations for much of their data collection. Especially in developing countries, the isolation of large segments of the population, pub-lic suspicion of government officials, language barriers, and outright political manipulation of the data can seriously undermine data reliability.

Sometimes, a statistic that is unreliable in cross-sectional comparisons may be reliable in time series comparisons and vice versa. Inconsistencies in how some (actually, just a few) countries count live births may result in a rela-tively higher reported U.S. infant mortality rate, but this would not explain why the U.S. rate is falling at a slower pace than other nations (figure 1.5).

Sampling Error   One source of measurement unreliability is sampling error—the degree to which estimates may be wrong due to the use of a sample rather than a complete count of the population. With the exception of data based on agency records, such as birth and death records, data on government budgets, and decennial census indicators based on counts of the whole population, almost all social indicator statistics are obtained from surveys of a relatively small sample of the targeted population. Most public opinion polling data are based on sample sizes ranging from 400 to 1,600 persons. U.S. government social indicators are often based on much larger sample sizes. The Current Pop-ulation Survey's monthly unemployment rate statistics are based on samples of 50,000 persons, and estimates of annual income, poverty rates, and health insurance coverage are based on surveys of 100,000 households.

Because not all of the population is surveyed, estimates derived from samples are not exact and are subject to a "sampling error," which depends for the most part on the sample size. Larger samples have less sampling

Figure 1.5. Infant Mortality Rates (per 1,000 live births), 22 Wealthy OECD Nations, 1960–2008 (log scale).

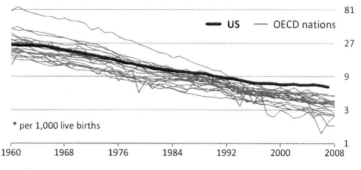

Source: OECD Health Data 2010.

error. For public opinion polling, sampling error can be estimated using this simple formula:[18]

$$sampling\ error = \frac{1}{\sqrt{N}} \times 100$$

For polls with a sample size (*N*) of 400, the sampling error is ±5 percent; for sample sizes of 1,600, it is 2.5 percent. Quadrupling the sample size reduces the error by half (table 1.2). This estimate of sampling error calculates the error for a 95 percent confidence interval. Thus, if a poll of 400 likely voters finds that 52 percent will vote for the Democratic candidate, we can be 95 percent confident that between 47 percent and 57 percent of the population of likely voters would have indicated that they would vote for the Democrat. How confident you can really be in such a number depends on how confident you can be in the poll's method of determining who the likely voters are. Polling organizations, however, rarely release this information.

TABLE 1.2

Sampling Error

Sample Size	Sample Error
100	10.0%
400	5.0%
900	3.3%
1600	2.5%
6400	1.3%

Sampling error—the errors in measurement caused by using a small sample to represent the whole population—is just one aspect of measurement reliability, and a highly overrated aspect at that. The estimate of a poll's margin of error is based on a premise that is almost always false: that the persons sampled constitute a random sample of the targeted population and that the persons who were sampled but did not take part in the survey are no different than those who did.

The seeming precision of the sampling error estimate belies all sorts of other sources of unreliability in sampling, particularly those caused by low response rates to the polls. Not everybody is at home when the surveyors appear at the door; many people do not have telephones; people with cell phones (often, college students) cannot be contacted even with the customary random-digit dialing; and many people simply refuse to answer the surveys. For these reasons, one should always be wary of the use of sampling error alone as a measure of the reliability of polling results.

Almost every newspaper story reporting the results of a public opinion poll contains a standard sentence indicating the sample size and that the poll has a "margin of error of plus or minus X percent." News stories hardly ever contain any information about the poll's response rate, a fact I confirmed by searching the Internet for the phrases commonly used in poll news stories (table 1.3). If election pollsters and their newspaper sponsors were to report response rates (the percentage of those they tried to contact who actually answered the questions), the public would know a lot more about the reliability of their polls than they do from the sampling error statistic.

The much larger polls used to derive estimates for many U.S. government social indicator estimates have much smaller sampling errors. Census Bureau unemployment and poverty estimates derived from the Current Population Survey report a .2 percentage point sampling error (using a

TABLE 1.3
Press Reporting of Polling Reliability

Search terms:	Search Engine News "Hits"		
	Bing	Yahoo!	Google
"plus or minus" poll	3,920	1,225	922
"plus or minus" survey	2,380	900	786
"margin of error" "plus or minus"	1,330	681	376
"response rate" poll	12	12	20
"response rate" survey	64	131	123

August 1, 2011

more liberal 90 percent confidence interval). The larger sample size is necessary to produce reliable estimates for subgroups of the sample. Governmental agencies also have much higher response rates: well over 90 percent for the monthly Current Population Survey. Most polling agencies would be happy with a 40 percent response rate.

RELIABILITY AND VALIDITY OF CRIME STATISTICS

In the 1930s, the Federal Bureau of Investigation (FBI) began collecting crime statistics, producing the Uniform Crime Report (UCR), a monthly index of violent and property crimes reported to the Bureau by federal, state, and local police agencies. For decades, the UCR data were regarded as the authoritative measure of the nation's crime rate, and the FBI worked with state and local agencies to ensure that the agencies followed consistent standards in classifying and reporting crimes. Nevertheless, there were serious questions about the reliability of the UCR crime measure. Not all crimes are reported to the police, and at least some police agencies lack the technical sophistication or the political incentive to tabulate all the crimes that are reported to them. These factors would combine to make it appear that the least competent and professional police agencies had lower crime rates. Over time, an increasing willingness of crime victims to report crimes to the police, particularly sexual assault, would also tend to make it appear that crime is increasing, when it is not.

Partly to correct these problems, in 1972 the Bureau of Justice Statistics began an annual public survey, the National Crime Victimization Survey (NCVS), of over 77,000 households to measure the incidence of rape, sexual assault, robbery, assault, theft, household burglary, and motor vehicle theft. Although the NCVS survey has some random sampling error and the samples are too small to produce reliable estimates for all but the nation's largest cities, it is a highly consistent measure of national crime trends and is regarded as more reliable than the FBI data. Nevertheless, problems remain with the reliability of NCVS crime estimates, and an unknown number of crimes still go unreported. Because one person in each household is asked to report the crimes committed against each member of the household, in cases where the person being interviewed has committed assaults against other family members, the crimes will probably go unrecorded.[19]

The nation's violent crime rates are the most commonly reported NCVS and UCR statistics. Because murder was not included in the survey (murder victims tend not to respond to surveys), the NCVS violent crime estimates include the UCR murder rate figure (which is assumed to be reliably reported) in its estimate of total violent crime. As we see in figure 1.6, the

Figure 1.6. Violent Crime Rates: FBI Uniform Crime Report and National Victimization Survey (per 1,000 population, age 12+).

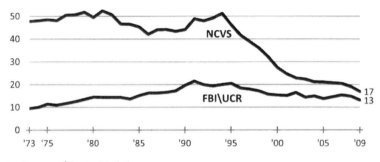

Source: Bureau of Justice Statistics.

two measures reveal quite different results. The UCR data indicate that the violent crime rate has increased 25 percent since 1973, while the NCVS estimate has declined by two-thirds.

Generally, researchers conclude that the true crime rate parallels the NCVS trend and that the UCR trend has not declined as dramatically because of better police department record keeping and a greater willingness among the public to report crimes to the police.

Similar questions of the reliability and validity of social indicators arise in the case of unemployment rate statistics. The Bureau of Labor Statistics provides two different employment statistics, one based on household surveys (similar to the NCVS survey) and another based on a payroll survey of business establishments. The household survey is the basis for the most commonly reported unemployment statistic, while the payroll survey provides a general measure of the health of the economy. In recent years (particularly from 2001 to 2003), the two numbers have diverged widely, with the household survey indicating much better economic news coming out of the post-9/11 recession. There are problems with the payroll survey because it is based on surveys from existing business establishments and does not count the self-employed. The household survey, on the other hand, suffers from nonresponse biases (for example, people who are paid in cash to avoid income taxes) and its reliance on "proxy responses" by household members.[20]

CHOOSING THE RIGHT INDICATOR

Choosing appropriate performance measures and basing decisions on numerical evidence is often the key to success in many realms of public and private affairs. While many business and government organizations use sound data to guide management decisions, many others combine weak data with faulty interpretations that usually confirm the wisdom of existing practices. And some of our most revered institutions avoid data-based decision making altogether, or reserve their data analysis to debunking the validity of any performance-based measurement. If you are reading this book for a college class, chances are that only you and your professor will know whether or not you have learned anything by the end of the course. Other professions use data to measure departmental and employee performance, product quality, customer satisfaction, and return on investments. Then they allocate resources and reward employees based on such evidence.

Figure 1.7a. Team Batting Average and Total Runs Scored, 2011 Season.

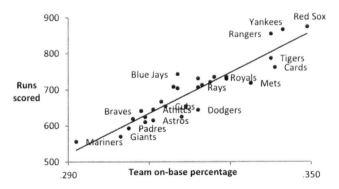

Source: MLB.com.

Figure 1.7b. On-Base Percentage and Total Runs Scored, 2011 Season.

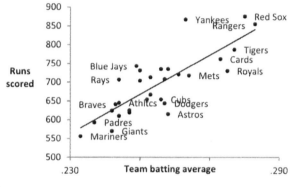

Source: MLB.com.

Perhaps no other institution in our society is as rich in data as baseball. Almost every baseball decision and argument about the game is at some point subject to statistical evidence. Does a sacrifice bunt make sense?[21] Is Ron Santo more deserving of the Hall of Fame than Phil Rizzuto?[22]

Baseball has always been data-rich, but in recent years baseball statistics have undergone a revolutionary expansion with the development of "sabermetrics" (named for the acronym of the Society for American Baseball Research), a whole new science of collecting and analyzing baseball data. Essentially, sabermetrics is just plain data analysis applied to baseball.

The use of sabermetrics is illustrated in the book and movie *Moneyball*, the story of the exploits of Billy Beane, general manager of the Oakland Athletics baseball team.[23] The premise of the story was that major league baseball scouts and executives made poor use of the statistics that were available to them in evaluating baseball talent and overrated players based on statistics such as stolen bases, runs batted in (RBIs), batting average, and the speed of a pitcher's fastball. Because the Athletics generally lacked the resources to pay for high-priced players, Beane sought out better measures of players' contributions to their teams' success and recruited players who were undervalued by the traditional wisdom.

One of these measures was a relatively new statistic, a batters-on-base percentage. As we can see in figures 1.7a and 1.7b, the on-base average is a better predictor of a team's ability to score runs than is the more traditional batting average. Bean sought out players with relatively low batting averages but high on-base averages.

Despite a player payroll of only $41 million, less than a third of the payroll of the New York Yankees,[24] Bean's use of sabermetrics is credited for the team's remarkable success in the early '00 decade. Unfortunately for Oakland, the publication of *Moneyball* exposed the team's trade secrets, and the wealthier teams are now using their financial resources to signing the previously undervalued players and to recruit their own sabermetricians.

NOTES

1. John Boehner quoted in David Lawder, "Boehner Vows to Repeal Obama Healthcare Reforms," Reuters, November 3, 2010, at http://www.reuters.com/article/2010/11/03/us-usa-elections-republicans-health-idUSTRE6A25DB20101103.

2. Staff of the *Washington Post*, *Landmark: The Inside Story of America's New Health Care Law and What It Means for Us All* (Philadelphia: PublicAffairs Books, 2010).

3. Central Intelligence Agency, *The World Factbook*, at https://www.cia.gov/library/publications/the-world-factbook/ (accessed June 10, 2011).

4. See, for example, Betsy McCaughey on *The Daily Show*, August 20, 2009, at http://www.thedailyshow.com/watch/thu-august-20-2009/betsy-mccaughey-pt-1.

5. Daniel Patrick Moynihan, quoted in Timothy J. Penny, "Facts Are Facts," *National Review*, September 4, 2003.

6. World Bank, *World Development Report 1993: Investing in Health*, vol. 1 (New York: Oxford University Press, 1993).

7. U.S. Arms Control and Disarmament Agency, *World Military Expenditures* (Washington, DC: Government Printing Office, 1971).

8. Ruth Leger Sivard, "Speech by Ms. Ruth Leger Sivard, Laureate of the UNESCO Prize 1991 for Peace Education" (Paris: UNESCO, 1992) at http://unesdoc.unesco.org/images/0012/001227/122733eo.pdf. The 1974 ACDA report says that the data were omitted "partly because of the paucity of data, but also because the omission of private health and education expenditures led to distorted comparisons between free market and centrally planned economies." See U.S. Arms Control and Disarmament Agency, *World Military Expenditures and Arms Trade* (Washington: Government Printing Office, 1974), iii.

9. Ruth Leger Sivard, *World Military and Social Expenditures 1974* (Washington, DC: World Priorities, 1974). Thanks to Jim Sivard (jimsivard@verizon.net) for information about his mother.

10. "Count, Divide, and Compare" is a formulation developed by epidemiologists at the Centers for Disease Control and Prevention (CDC).

11. National Commission on Excellence in Education, *A Nation at Risk: The Imperative for Educational Reform*, April 1983, at http://www.ed.gov/pubs/NatAtRisk.

12. Michael E. Mann, Raymond S. Bradley, and Malcolm K. Hughes, "Global-Scale Temperature Patterns and Climate Forcing over the Past Six Centuries," *Nature* 392:779–87. Mann, Bradley, and Hughes's original charts were based on reconstruction of temperatures over six hundred years; the data in figure 1.2 are regarded as more reliable data based on meteorological station records.

13. See National Center for Fair and Open Testing (FairTest), at http://www.fairtest.org; Nicholas Lemann, *The Big Test: The Secret History of the American Meritocracy* (New York: Farrar, Straus & Giroux, 1999).

14. Robert D. Putnam, *Bowling Alone: The Collapse and Revival of American Community* (New York: Simon & Schuster, 2000).

15. World Health Organization, *The World Health Report 2000—Health Systems: Improving Performance* (Geneva: World Health Organization, 2000).

16. Morris David Morris, *Measuring the Conditions of the World's Poor: The Physical Quality of Life Index* (New York: Pergamon, 1979).

17. U.S. Census Bureau Public Information Office, "Statement of Census Bureau Director C. Louis Kincannon on Accuracy and Coverage Evaluation Revision II," U.S. Department of Commerce News, March 12, 2003 (CB03-CS.02), at http://www.census.gov/Press-Release/www/releases/archives/directors_corner/000813.html.

18. The basic equation for sampling error was "discovered" by Abraham De Moivre, *Miscellanea Analytica* (London: Tonson and Watts, 1730). A more complicated formula provides more precise estimates and should be used when the size of the population, or the sample percentage, is relatively small.

19. Michael R. Rand and Callie M. Rennison, "True Crime Stories? Accounting for Differences in Our National Crime Indicators," *Chance Magazine* 15, no. 1 (Winter 2002): 47–51.

20. Tao Wu, "Two Measures of Employment: How Different Are They?" Federal Reserve Bank of San Francisco Economic Letter Number 2004–23, August 27, 2004, 1–3, at http://frbsf.org/publications/economics/letter/2004/el2004-23.html.

21. The evidence suggests the sacrifice bunt is usually a bad idea. With a runner on first and no outs, teams average .919 runs per inning. With a runner on second and one out, they average .707 runs. See John Thorn and Pete Palmer, *The Hidden Game of Baseball* (Garden City, NY: Doubleday, 1985).

22. World Series Championships: Rizzuto, 7; Santo, 0. Radio catchphrases: Rizzuto, "Holy cow!" (as the Yankees hit another home run); Santo, "Oh NOOOO!" (as the Cubs bullpen blows another one).

23. Michael Lewis, *Moneyball: The Art of Winning an Unfair Game* (New York: Norton, 2004).

24. Complaints about the Yankees' high payrolls are most unfair and do not take into account the higher cost of living in New York City.

CHAPTER 2

Measuring Racial and Ethnic Inequality

> Yes, but the numbers I have are very true, and even if some people
> think I am not black enough for them, the numbers speak for
> themselves.
>
> —BILL COSBY

BILL COSBY is wrong: Numbers never speak for themselves, but the point he is trying to make is entirely valid. Cosby was responding to critics of his controversial speech at the 2004 NAACP gala commemorating the fiftieth anniversary of the *Brown v. Board of Education* decision. Cosby was accused of hypocrisy, embracing inauthentic middle-class values, expressing contempt for the plight of the black poor, coddling white audiences, and lending aid to those who really do not care about black America.[1] Had Cosby responded in kind—as many talk show hosts who embraced his remarks did—the media frenzy that ensued might have been more entertaining. Instead, he responded with a book, coauthored with Alvin F. Poussaint, challenging his critics to account for a litany of statistics describing the lives of young black men in America.[2] The statistics he cites, rates of black male murder, crime, imprisonment, dropping out of high school, unemployment, life expectancy, and homelessness, point to serious problems confronting the black community and American society.[3] By themselves, the numbers do not suggest a particular course of action or necessarily support any of the solutions Cosby offers, but by shifting the focus of attention from his own motives to the numerical evidence, Cosby moved the debate in a positive direction.

For the United States, the most disturbing social indicator comparisons are often those that involve race. In almost every American field of study where social indicators are used, race and ethnicity are among the most commonly used demographic comparisons. This chapter will illustrate the scope

23

and breadth of social indicator data that address issues of racial and ethnic disparities in poverty and income, health, education, and criminal justice.

MEASURING RACE AND ETHNICITY

The U.S. Census Bureau and almost all federal statistical agencies differ from the bureaus and agencies of most other countries in that the United States classifies people by race and not by religion.[4] The French Census is forbidden by law to ask questions related to race, ethnicity, or religion, but most other countries use classifications based on nationality, national origin, and ethnicity. The United States is one of very few countries that treats race and ethnicity as two separate classifications. In the past, the Census Bureau divided race into four general categories: American Indian or Alaskan Native, Asian or Pacific Islander, black, and white. Often these were reported as just white, black, and other. Ethnicity, most commonly divided into "Hispanic" and "non-Hispanic," is a separate classification, asked as a separate question on the Census forms. Thus one may see the phrase "Hispanics may be of any race" as a footnote to many U.S. government statistical tables. Alternatively, the data may be cross-classified as "white-non-Hispanic, black, Asian, and Hispanic."

This all became more complicated when, beginning with the 2000 Census, the Bureau added the category of "Native Hawaiian or Other Pacific Islander" to the race category (table 2.1), and persons were allowed to classify themselves as more than one race. Because of the multiple race combinations, we now see statistics reported for groups defined by categories such as "black-alone" and "black-alone-or-in-combination." The changes allowed for over one hundred possible ethnic and multiple-racial classifications, but it is rare that more than seven categories are used in reports and tabulations. Depending on what data are available, the simplest solution to this problem, and one that seems to provide the most consistent estimates before and after the 2000 Census, is to count as Hispanics all those, regardless of race, who indicate that they are Hispanic; to report whites as those who are neither Hispanic nor a combination of races (reported by the Census as "Non-Hispanic, white alone"); to classify as black those who indicate that they are black if they have chosen more than one race ("Non-Hispanic, black-alone-or-in-combination"); and for Asians, non-Hispanic Asians who have chosen only one race ("Non-Hispanic, Asian alone").

The Hispanics became the nation's largest "minority" group in 2001 and comprised just over 16 percent of the entire population in 2009. Given the rise of anti-Muslim sentiments in the United States after 9/11, it is noteworthy that because the Census does not count religion, there are no Census

TABLE 2.1

Population by Race and Ethnicity, 2009

	(millions)			
	One race	One or more races	Not Hispanic	Hispanic
White	244	249	200	44
Black	40	42	38	2
Asian	14	16	14	0
American Indian*	4	6	3	1
Total	**302**	**312**	**259**	**48**
	Percent of entire population			
White	78	80	64	14
Black	13	13	12	1
Asian	4	5	4	0
American Indian*	1	2	1	0
Total	**97**	**100**	**83**	**16**

* also includes Alaskan Native, Hawaiian and Pacific Islander
Source: Census Bureau, Population Division

figures on the nation's Muslim population. The Census did count 1.2 million American as of Arab ancestry in 2000 (but note that a majority of U.S. Arab Americans are Christian). The Pew Research Center estimates the U.S. Muslim population at 2.6 million.[5]

INCOME AND WEALTH

The Census Bureau's *Current Population Survey* (CPS), conducted with the Bureau of Labor Statistics, provides numerous measures of earnings and employment status for individuals, families, households, and members of the labor force. The March CPS survey, the Annual Social and Economic Supplement (the CPS ASEC) is a larger survey of 100,000 households and is the primary source for data on annual income, poverty, and health insurance coverage.

We will see in chapter 9 (table 9.2, figure 9.4) that among industrialized nations, the United States has extremely high levels of poverty and economic inequality. The Census Bureau classified more than a quarter of black and Hispanic families with children as poor in 2009: their family income fell below the Census Bureau poverty threshold (for a family of four, $22,050). Conservatives, and to some extent Cosby, place the blame for the high rates of black poverty and other inequalities on the proportion of families headed by single parents. It is true that the black poverty rate would otherwise be much lower (see table 9.3), but the black-white poverty gap remains large even among two-parent families. Hispanic poverty rates, on the other hand, are almost as high as the black rates, despite much lower rates of both single-parent families and unemployment.

Differences in education account for some but not all of the black-white and Hispanic-white income and earnings gaps. Black men and women earn about a third less than whites, but the income gap is reduced by about half when comparing persons of the same level of education.

The racial income inequalities pale in comparison to the racial gaps in net household worth, which measures savings and assets such as home equity. The wealth gap reached a record high in 2009 (table 2.2), with the

TABLE 2.2

Income, Poverty and Unemployment, by Race and Ethnicity,* 2009

	White*	Black	Hispanic	Black\White ratio
Poverty rate, families:				
all families with children	11	30	28	2.8
two-parent families	5	13	21	2.5
%Children in single-parent families	21	61	35	2.8
Unemployment rates (2008)				
age 16+	5	10	8	1.9
age 16-19	17	31	22	1.9
median earnings:				
full time, year-round workers:				
men	51,400	31,400	37,500	0.61
women	38,500	27,000	32,000	0.70
highest educational attainment: (2006)				
Less than high school	25,400	21,300	21,100	0.84
High school graduate	31,500	25,400	25,400	0.81
Bachelor's degree	44,700	38,600	40,600	0.86
Master's degree	50,800	45,700	48,800	0.90
Net household wealth: (2009$)				
2005	135,000	12,000	18,000	0.13
2009	113,000	5,677	6,325	0.06

*White: "Non Hispanic, white alone"; Black: "black alone or in combination"; Hispanic: of any race

Sources: Census Bureau, Bureau of Labor Statistics, National Center for Education Statistics, Pew Research Center

median worth of white households 20 times that of black households (compared to 11 times in 2005). In just four years, black net worth had declined by more than half and Hispanic net worth by nearly two-thirds. And this was only one year into the Great Recession.

Researchers often use family income as a control variable to assess whether or not it accounts for disparities in other indicators such as health status, educational achievement, or mortgage approval. The research typically finds that racial and ethnic disparities persist even when comparing whites, blacks, and Hispanics of the same income. Such research, however, doesn't take into account the often large racial and ethnic disparities in family wealth among groups with the same level of income. Because net wealth is less frequently recorded than family income by the Census, and even more rarely in other government and private surveys, it is a factor that much research does not take into account.

HEALTH

Much of the nation's health care data are provided through the Centers for Disease Control and Prevention's (CDC) National Center for Health Statistics (NCHS). Most of the NCHS data related to births and mortality are provided through the National Vital Statistics System and are based on information collected from local and state government birth, death, and marriage records. The CDC also collects a great deal of other data from national health surveys and surveys of health care providers.

As we saw earlier, the United States has the lowest life expectancy and highest infant mortality rates among wealthy OECD nations (figures 1.4 and 1.5). If Black America were a country, it would rank 94th in infant mortality (close to Jamaica and Tonga) and 120th in life expectancy (just slightly better than Latvia and Egypt) (table 2.3).[6]

Although there is an extensive literature tying African American health outcomes to access to medical and prenatal care, poverty, teenage pregnancy, and high rates of obesity,[7] the data for Hispanics present a perplexing anomaly. Hispanics and blacks have about the same poverty rates, almost identical teenage pregnancy rates, similar obesity rates, and Hispanics are much less likely than any group to be covered by health insurance. Nevertheless, Hispanics have both lower infant mortality rates and longer life expectancy than whites.

Epidemiologists who have studied the "Hispanic Anomaly" (or "Latino Paradox") have questioned the reliability of these data.[8] Could immigrant

TABLE 2.3
Health Status by Race and Ethnicity

	White	Black	Hispanic	Black\White ratio
Infant mortality rate* 2006	5.6	13.4	5.4	2.4
Teenage pregnancy rate** 2006	44	126	127	2.9
Life expectancy, 2006:				
at birth	77.6	72.9	80.6	0.9
at age 65	18.5	17.0	20.6	0.9
Obesity rates:				
adults, 2009	25.6	38.1	31.7	1.5
boys, age 12-19, 2006-8	16.7	19.8	26.8	1.2
girls, age 12-19, 2006-8	14.5	29.2	17.4	2.0
Elevated blood lead levels >10 µg /dL, 1999-02				
age 1-5	1.3	3.1	2.0***	2.4
age 60+	0.4	3.4	1.8***	8.5
% uninsured, 2010	11.7	20.8	30.7	1.8

*infant mortality: per 1,000 births
**pregnancy: per 1,000 teenage women
*** Mexican-American
Sources: National Center for Health Statistics, Gutmacher Institute, Center for Disease Control, Census Bureau

deaths be underreported? Is the recording of Hispanic ethnicity on death certificates consistent with the Census recording of the Hispanic population? (The Census's Hispanic classification is based on self-reporting in Census surveys, an option that is generally unavailable at the time of death.) Are unhealthy immigrants, or women with unhealthy newborns, more likely to return to their native countries? In the case of infant mortality (the data on Hispanic life expectancy are too recent for extensive study), there has been a great deal of speculation, but no satisfactory explanation has been found: Infant mortality for Mexican-immigrant women is about 10 percent lower than white infant mortality even at one hour, one day, and one week after birth.[9]

Exposure to lead has diminished greatly in recent decades due to federal bans on leaded gas and lead paint and restrictions on industrial pollution in the 1970s (France, Belgium, and Austria banned lead paint in 1909). Childhood exposure to lead, primarily through exposure to the paint and lead in plumbing fixtures in older homes, results in many chronic health conditions, impairs mental development, and is associated with learning disabilities and behavioral disorders. As noted in chapter 4, there is some intriguing evidence connecting childhood lead exposure to high levels of crime.

EDUCATION

National data on educational attainment are most often provided through the *Current Population Survey* (CPS), but data on educational achievement, as well as data related to state and local educational institutions' spending, staffing, enrollment, and graduation, are provided by the National Center for Education Statistics (NCES). The most comprehensive and detailed data on student learning are provided through the NCES's National Assessment of Educational Progress, based on tests of national samples of students in grades 4, 8, and 12 (or ages 9, 13, and 17) in math, science, and reading—and less frequently in arts, civics, economics, geography, and U.S. history (table 2.4).

As we will see in chapter 8, the United States generally ranks poorly on international measures of education achievement (see figure 8.1), and the racial and ethnic gaps in learning account for a great deal of the U.S. performance. Despite an enormous research effort and educational policies and reforms designed to close the achievement gap, the United States has made little progress in addressing the inequalities. On both math and reading exams, black students nearing high school graduation consistently show levels of achievement equivalent to white eighth graders.

As we will see in chapter 8, there is an extensive literature on racial gaps in learning and considerable debate over whether the causes can be traced to racial discrimination, differences in school resources, differences in family economic background, or students' home environments.

The percentage of 25- to-29-year-olds who have completed high school is the inverse measure of the high school "status-dropout" rate. Thus we can calculate that the black student dropout rate is twice the white rate, while the Hispanic rate is six times higher. One critic of Bill Cosby's speech, Michael Eric Dyson,[10] citing a 17 percent black dropout rate based on a 2003 source, took particular offense at Cosby's claim that "in our cities and public schools we have fifty percent drop out." There has been some improvement in black high school dropout rates in recent years, falling from 19 percent

TABLE 2.4
Education Indicators by Race and Ethnicity

	White	Black	Hispanic	Black\White ratio
% below basic, NAEP math				
4th grade, 2009	9	36	29	4.0
8th grade, 2009	17	50	43	2.9
12th grade, 2005	30	70	60	2.3
Average math scale score, 2008				
4th grade	250	224	234	
8th grade	290	262	268	
12th grade, 2005	314	287	293	
Time spent on school days, 4th graders, 2000				
homework: 1 hour or more	47	46	38	1.0
watching TV: 6 hours or more	18	46	27	2.6
% of 25-29-year-olds, 2009:				
completed high school	95	90	69	0.9
completed some college	69	55	37	0.8
bachelors degree or higher	39	19	14	0.5

Source: National Center for Education Statistics

in 1980 to 10 percent in 2009 (based on the 90 percent completing high school in table 2.4), but part of the decline is due to the doubling of the black male incarceration rate. The Current Population Survey is based on a survey of the noninstitutionalized population. In effect, the Census does not count any of the more than 10 percent of black males aged 25 to 29 who are in jail or prison as dropouts (or graduates). Because high school graduation rates (and thus dropout rates) and many other CPS indicators such as poverty and unemployment are based on surveys of the noninstitutionalized population, black males are disproportionately excluded from the data, and many of the racial gaps in such indicators are greater than the statistics indicate. Cosby responded to Dyson with evidence that in many large cities the black male dropout rate does indeed exceed 50 percent. These data are often based on counts of the number of students who graduate divided by the number of students in attendance four years earlier.

The United States has been steadily falling behind other nations in both high school and college graduation rates (table 6.4, figure 8.2). Comparing the percentage of each group that has attended some college with the percentage that has attained a degree we can see that the racial and ethnic disparities in college graduation rates are substantial.

CRIME AND PUNISHMENT

As we saw in chapter 1, since 1930, the FBI has compiled statistics on crime and crime rates in its Uniform Crime Reporting program, based on data collected from state and local police agencies. During the Nixon administration, the Bureau of Justice Statistics was created to provide more comprehensive data on the nation's criminal justice system, including, since 1973, the National Crime Victimization Survey (NCVS), based (in 2008) on a sample of 76,000 households and 135,000 persons.

Of all the social indicators measuring racial inequality, except wealth, the greatest disparities have to do with the high rate of incarceration of black males (table 2.5). The Unites States, as a whole, imprisons a higher percentage of its population than any other nation in the world, and the

TABLE 2.5
Crime and Punishment

	White	Black	Hispanic	Black\White ratio
Imprisonment* rate, males, 2008	0.7	4.8	1.8	6.6
Lifetime likelihood of going to prison, males, 2001	5.9	32.1	17.2	5.4
Violent crime victimization rate, 2008 per 1,000 population, age 12 years+	18.1	25.9	16.4	1.4

Composition of White and Black Population:**		
	% White	% Black
Total population, 2008	86	14
Violent crime victims, 2008	82	18
Violent crime offenders, 2008	72	28
Murder victims, 2009	50	50
Murder offenders, 2009	47	53
Jail and prison inmates, 2008	46	54
Death row inmates 2009	56	42

*prisons and jails
**includes Hispanics
Source: Bureau of Justice Statistics, Federal Bureau of Investigation

black imprisonment rates are six times that of the general population. The rates of incarceration for blacks and the population as a whole have historically been high, but a wave of state and federal laws in the 1970s and 1980s involving mandatory minimum sentences, "three strikes and you're out" (lifetime imprisonment for a third felony conviction), and the war on drugs greatly increased the prison population. Between 1980 and 2009, the U.S. prison population increased from 320,000 to over 1.5 million, and imprisonment for nonviolent drug offenses went from 19,000 to over 275,000.[11] Approximately half of the prison population is black.

Based on 2001 incarceration rates, the Bureau of Justice Statistics estimates that over 30 percent of black males will spend some of their life in state or federal prison (and this does not count time spent in jail for less-than-felony convictions). The incarceration rate disparity is partly attributable to higher black crime rates, but in the case of imprisonment for drug offenses, the connection between offenses and imprisonment is stark: Most studies show that whites and blacks are about equally likely to use drugs, yet blacks are far more likely to serve time for drug offenses.

Since 2003, both the FBI and the NCVS have reported hate crime statistics, much the same way each agency reports other crimes. The FBI hate crime data are highly unreliable, however, due to the wide discretion local agencies have in reporting the crimes, and the NCVS data are subjective in that they are based on the victim's suspicion of the offender's motives. Although nearly 90 percent of the hate crime victimizations involved suspected racial or ethnic motivations, they account for less than 1 percent of all reported victimizations. Surprisingly, whites and blacks report equal hate crime victimization rates (.6 per 1,000). The Hispanic rate is somewhat higher at .9 per 1,000 of population.[12]

The mass incarceration of young males has severe social, economic, and even political effects on urban black communities. The high rates of felony convictions are both cause and effect of both the high unemployment rates and the high rates of single-parent families in black communities.[13] Those incarcerated for nonviolent drug offenses are more likely to become violent offenders after they are released.[14] Because of state laws that often bar convicted felons from voting, 13 percent of adult black males are disenfranchised.[15]

THE SEARCH FOR SOLUTIONS

On most of these indicators, there has been little or no improvement in the racial and ethnic disparities over the past several decades. Much of the debate focuses on theory and research that attempts to identify the under-lying causes of the inequality, whether it be racism, culture, or ineffective social policies. Even with that, finding a cause is not the same thing as find-ing a solution.

Part of the problem is that many of the inequities are both cause and effect of each other. Children in single-parent families do poorly in school and are more likely to end up unemployed or in prison. On the other hand, the high rates of imprisonment and unemployment are likely causes of the high rates of children being born into single-parent families.[16]

NOTES

1. Michael Eric Dyson, *Is Bill Cosby Right? Or Has the Black Middle Class Lost Its Mind?* (New York: Basic Civitas Books, 2005).

2. Bill Cosby and Alvin F. Poussaint, *Come On People: On the Path from Victims to Victors* (Nashville, TN: Thomas Nelson, 2007), xv.

3. Cosby and Poussaint, *Come On People*, 8–9.

4. Hate crime statistics are one exception to this rule; religious hate crimes are clas-sified as anti Jewish, Catholic, Protestant, Islamic, other, and atheist.

5. Pew Research Center, "The Future of the Global Muslim Population: Projec-tions for 2010–2030," Pew Research Center Forum on Religion and Public Life, at http://pewforum.org/The-Future-of-the-Global-Muslim-Population.aspx (accessed January 27, 2011); G. Patricia de la Cruz and Angela Brittingham, "The Arab Population: 2000," U.S. Census 2000 Brief, December 2003, at http://www.census.gov/prod/2003pubs/c2kbr-23.pdf.

6. U.S. Central Intelligence Agency, *The World Factbook*, at https://www.cia.gov/library/publications/the-world-factbook/ (accessed November 24, 2011).

7. Ichiro Kawachi, Norman Daniels, and Dean E. Robinson, "Health Disparities by Race and Class: Why Both Matter," *Health Affairs* 24, no. 2 (2005): 343–52.

8. Kyriakos S. Markides and Jeannine Coreil, "The Health of Hispanics in the South-western United States: An Epidemiologic Paradox," *Public Health Reports* 101, no. 3 (May–June 1986): 253–65, at http://www.ncbi.nlm.nih.gov/pmc/articles/PMC1477704/pdf/pubhealthrep00183-0027.pdf.

9. Robert A. Hummer, Daniel A. Powers, Starling G. Pullum, et al., "Paradox Found (Again): Infant Mortality among the Mexican-Origin Population in the United States," *Demography* 44, no. 3 (August 2007): 441–57, at http://www.jstor.org/stable/30053096.

10. Dyson, *Is Bill Cosby Right?* 71.

11. Lauren E. Glaze, "Correctional Populations in the United States, 2009," *Bureau of Justice Statistics Bulletin*, December 2010, NCJ 231681, at http://bjs.ojp.usdoj.gov/index.cfm?ty=pbdetail&iid=2316.

12. Lynn Langton and Micheal Planty, "Hate Crime, 2003–2009," *Bureau of Justice Statistics Special Report*, June 2011, NCJ 234085, at http://bjs.ojp.usdoj.gov/content/pub/pdf/hc0309.pdf.

13. William J. Wilson, *More Than Just Race: Being Black and Poor in the Inner City* (New York: Norton, 2009).

14. Michelle Alexander, *The New Jim Crow: Mass Incarceration in the Age of Color-blindness* (New York: New Press, 2011).

15. The Sentencing Project, "Felony Disenfranchisement Laws in the United States," March 2011, at http://www.sentencingproject.org/template/page.cfm?id=133.

16. William Julius Wilson, *The Declining Significance of Race: Blacks and Changing American Institutions* (Chicago: University of Chicago Press, 2012).

CHAPTER 3

Statistical Fallacies, Paradoxes, and Threats to Validity

Shallow men believe in luck. Strong men believe in cause and effect.
—RALPH WALDO EMERSON

A N ARGUMENT, as defined by those who study rhetoric and public discourse, is a series of statements, called premises, that are offered to support a conclusion. The premises of an argument consist of statements of fact and evidence, assumptions, and other reasons for believing the conclusion. An invalid argument, or an argument based on a logical fallacy, is one in which the premises, even if they are true, provide weak or insufficient support for the conclusion. Since Aristotle, philosophers have identified a great many logical fallacies common in public discourse. The *ad hominem* fallacy, for example, asserts the falsehood of a conclusion based on the motives or character of the author (President Obama's father came from Kenya, therefore Obamacare is un-American). The *post hoc, ergo propter hoc* fallacy (Latin for "after this, therefore because of this") asserts that an event that occurs before another event is the cause (the rooster crowed; the sun rose; therefore, the rooster made the sun rise). Appeals to authority (97 percent of scientists believe that global warming is man-made, therefore it is), appeals to the majority (75 percent of Americans support the Second Amendment, therefore we should not have gun control), and appeals to loyalty (we should support our troops and not cut off funds for the war) contain premises which, by themselves, are not sufficient to support the direct conclusion. Other logical fallacies include slippery slope arguments, the straw man, begging the question, a red herring, and hasty generalization.

Statistical fallacies are a subset of logical fallacies common in arguments that are premised on numerical evidence, most commonly, in arguments that draw causal conclusions from numerical comparisons.

EVALUATING CAUSAL RELATIONSHIPS

Observed relationships based on social indicator comparisons across jurisdictions, time, and demographic groups provide direct evidence in support of descriptive conclusions about social phenomena. Comparing poverty rates, for example, the evidence of observed relationships would support the following descriptive conclusions:

- Child poverty rates in the United States are higher than in any other industrialized democracy (table 9.2; figure 9.4).
- The U.S. poverty rates fell during the Clinton administration, then rose during the Bush administration (figure 9.7).
- Poverty rates are higher for African American families than for white families (table 9.3).

The most important, crucial, and problematic uses of social indicator comparisons are when observed relationships are used as premises to support conclusions about causal relationships. Thus, the same poverty rate relationships that supported these descriptive conclusions might be used to draw these causal conclusions:

- American child poverty rates are high because the United States lacks the family-oriented social welfare programs common in European nations.
- Clinton administration tax and welfare policies led to a reduction in poverty rates.
- Racial disparities in U.S. poverty rates are a consequence of systemic American racism and discrimination.

Moving from evidence of a relationship that supports a descriptive conclusion to drawing a conclusion that implies causation usually requires both additional statistical evidence and a whole lot of reasoning and analysis. Data are just one part of causal arguments; no amount of empirical evidence alone is sufficient to support a claim that any social phenomenon is caused by something else. Ideally, causal claims are grounded in well-reasoned theoretical arguments and are supported by examples and illustrations in addition to the data that define the relationship.

A *spurious relationship* occurs when an observed relationship between two variables is not a causal relationship but is due to the effect of a third variable (or set of variables). The possibility that some other variables account for observed relationships is the reason why we have social scientists. Physical scientists have a convenient method for discounting the possibility that some other factors account for the relationships that they observe: the experiment. More often than not, social scientists who would conduct experiments find themselves under severe constraints. It would be hard to design a controlled experiment to determine whether single parenthood is a cause of poverty or whether the death penalty deters crime.

Following are illustrations of a number of statistical fallacies common in the interpretation of social indicator data. Several of these have been compiled in the work of Donald T. Campbell and his coauthors as "threats to internal validity," or potential alternative explanations for causal conclusions in research findings.[1]

Cherry Picking

Cherry picking, the selective culling of evidence to support a claim, is a common problem in political debate and social science research. Both sides in the "the American health care system is the best in the world" debate selected the best evidence they could find to support their arguments. In 2009, critics of global warming examined the data depicted in figure 1.2. Comparing the rate of increase in global temperatures in the 1980s, 1990s, and 2000s, they argued that "global warming is slowing down."[2] The other side saw the same data and argued that the latest decade had been the "warmest on record."[3] Cherry picking is compounded as people have a tendency to more carefully scrutinize data that conflict with their preconceived assumptions and to readily accept data that support their position.

With time series analysis, cherry picking often involves comparisons with arbitrary beginning and ending time points. Many of the claims that tax cuts actually result in increasing government revenues, based on an economic theory known as the Laffer curve, often cite evidence of improving economic performance and rising revenues over a period of time following the Reagan tax cuts of 1982.

In 1981, Congress and the Reagan administration enacted the biggest tax cuts in U.S. history, reducing the top marginal rate from 70 percent in 1981 to 50 percent in 1982.[4] Proponents of what was called "Reaganomics" often credit the tax cuts for the economic growth of the 1980s and the growth in federal government revenues in the 1980s. Heritage Foundation economist Daniel Mitchell argues the point: "Once the economy received an unambiguous tax cut in January 1983, income tax revenues climbed dramatically, increasing by more than 54 percent by 1989 (28 percent after

Figure 3.1a. Income Tax Revenues after Reagan Tax Cut, Cumulative % Change.

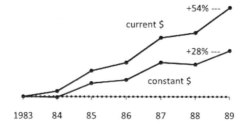

Source: 2012 Federal Budget, Historical Tables.

Figure 3.1b. Income Tax Revenues after Tax Changes, Cumulative % Change (constant $).

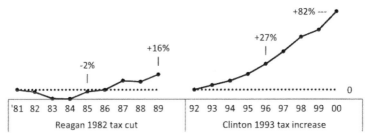

adjusting for inflation)."[5] As we see in figure 3.1a, Mitchell is correct; there was a significant increase in income tax revenues after the tax cut.

Note that although Mitchell acknowledges that the tax cut was fully in effect for the 1983 fiscal year, he measures the change that took place after 1983, ignoring the change the took place from 1982 to 1983. Although the general practice for measuring the effect of a policy change is "before and after," Mitchell has chosen an "after and longer after" approach. He also ignores that the tax cut was in effect for the last 9 months of fiscal year 1982. This excludes from his percentage increase calculation two years (or 21 months) of declining income tax revenue while the policy was in effect. Had he chosen 1981 as the base year—the year before the tax cuts went into effect—the revenue increases would not be as dramatic: in inflation-adjusted dollars, revenues increased just 16 percent (figure 3.1b). And it wasn't until 1986 that federal income tax revenues returned to the level they had been in 1981.

Mitchell also fails to note the economic growth and increased revenue that followed the 1993 Clinton tax increases, evidence that liberals often cite to counter the conservative claims. Mitchell did know about Clinton's tax increase: one week after Congress passed the legislation, he condemned it as the "largest tax increase in world history" and predicted that it "will lead to higher spending, larger deficits, more unemployment, and lower economic growth."[6] In fact, the Clinton tax increase was followed by the first budget surpluses in thirty years, surpluses that lasted until George W. Bush cut taxes in 2001.

History

"History," or historical events, is a broad category of third-variable causes that might be the cause of spurious relationships. Particularly when one is drawing a causal conclusion from a trend for a single program or administration, other historical events might account for the results.

The very good economic performance after the Clinton 1993 tax increases could be credited to the dot-com boom of the 1990s, to the Republicans gaining control of the Congress in 1995, or to a general improvement in the economy worldwide. Just as supporters of President Obama blame President Bush for the poor economic performance in 2009, 2010, and 2011, supporters of President Reagan blamed Carter administration policies for the first three years of the Reagan administration.

Reverse Causation

Fallacies of the "the rooster crowed, therefore the sun rose" type are more common in public debate than one might expect, as it is often not clear which of two variables in a relationship is cause and which is effect. Death penalty states, for example, actually have higher murder rates than non–death penalty states. Is this because the death penalty fosters more violence in society, or is it that more violent states tend to adopt the death penalty?

Political scientists have long hypothesized that higher voter turnout and more competitive elections lead to more responsive and better government. Low voter turnout fosters machine politics and corrupt government.[7] The relationship depicted in figure 3.2 would seem to support this theory: States with the highest levels of voter turnout tend to have lower rates of politicians being prosecuted for political corruption. Aside from the use of the prosecution rate as a measure of a state's level of political corruption (there may be high levels of corruption but very few prosecutions), the relationship might be due to reverse causation. High levels of political corruption might serve to lower voter turnout.

Figure 3.2. Voter Turnout and State Political Corruption.

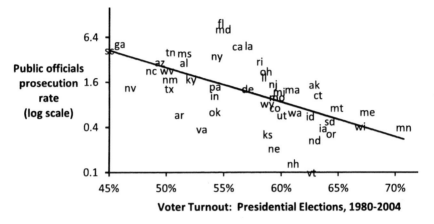

Source: US Elections Project; Schlesinger and Meier (2002).

Self-Selection

In March of 2011, Scott Gottlieb, a professor at New York University School of Medicine, published an opinion column in the *Wall Street Journal* under the headline, "Medicaid Is Worse Than No Coverage at All."[8] Gottlieb reported, "Dozens of recent medical studies show that Medicaid patients suffer for it. In some cases, they'd do just as well without health insurance." Several of the studies he summarized found that Medicaid patients with specific conditions (e.g., head and neck cancer) or undergoing specific treatments (e.g., lung transplant, coronary angioplasty) had substantially worse health outcomes than private patients with the same conditions or undergoing the same procedures. One of the studies found that in the case of major surgical procedures "uninsured patients were about 25 percent less likely than those with Medicaid to have an 'in-hospital death.'"

The last finding was based on a study that found that Medicaid patients had higher in-hospital mortality rates than uninsured patients for five of eight major surgical procedures and mortality rates twice as high as privately insured patients (table 3.1).[9]

The potential problem with such studies is that the comparison groups, Medicaid patients and privately insured or uninsured patients, may be dissimilar to begin with due to the phenomenon of self-selection. It is likely that many patients only enroll in Medicaid after, sometimes long after, a serious medical condition has developed. In this case, those who choose to enroll in Medicaid may be sicker than those who have private insurance or those who

TABLE 3.1

In-Hospital Mortality for Patients Undergoing Major Surgical Operations, by Primary Payer Group

Procedure	Private Insurance	Uninsured	Medicaid
Lung resection	2.0%	6.2%	4.3%
Esophagectomy	3.0%	6.5%	7.5%
Colectomy	1.8%	3.9%	5.4%
Pancreatectomy	2.7%	8.4%	5.8%
Gastrectomy	3.5%	5.0%	5.4%
Abdominal aneurysm	7.0%	14.8%	14.5%
Hip replacement	0.1%	0.1%	0.2%
Coronary bypass	1.4%	2.3%	2.8%

Source: Damien J. LaPar et.al., *Annals of Surgery* 252(3): 544–551.

are uninsured. In a sense, this self-selection effect is a form of reverse causation: Being sick causes people to enroll in Medicaid, not the reverse.

For a team of health care economists, a fiscal crisis in Oregon in 2008 provided a rare opportunity to measure the effect of Medicaid with an experiment.[10] Because of budget constraints, Oregon found itself with a Medicaid waiting list of ninety thousand people and only enough money to cover ten thousand of them. So the state created a lottery to randomly select people for enrollment, thus creating the necessary preconditions for a true experiment.

The results of the study were uniformly positive. In comparison to the control group that lost the lottery, Amy Finkelstein et al. wrote,

the treatment group had substantively and statistically significantly higher health care utilization (including primary and preventive care as well as hospitalizations), lower out-of-pocket medical expenditures and medical debt (including fewer bills sent to collection), and better self-reported physical and mental health.[11]

Unfortunately, the study still suffered from a self-selection problem. Many of the lottery winners were either not eligible for Medicaid or chose not to submit their paperwork to enroll in the program. The overall response rate was only 30 percent. Because the control group did not submit any paperwork, it is not known in what respects they might differ from the eventual treatment group. In all likelihood, because those who self-selected to participate in the experiment were probably sicker than those who did not, this self-selection might be expected to make Medicaid look worse. Without additional data, however, that cannot be tested. The experiment could have been fixed by requiring all the lottery participants (even those who would lose) to submit their paperwork before they knew the lottery results, thus excluding from both the treatment and control groups those who did not respond or were ineligible.

Sample Mortality

Sample mortality is the inverse of self-selection and often occurs when the participants who are doing most poorly in an experimental program drop out of the study. Many school voucher, charter school, and public school choice programs that enroll students in private or semiprivate schools use a lottery to select students for enrollment. When students at these schools do well on educational tests, a common complaint of school choice opponents is that the poorest or poorest-performing students tend to drop out of the programs and go back to their public school, lowering the public school scores and increasing the private school scores.

Maturation

Sometimes performance measures increase merely because the subjects have become older over the course of the study. Some indicators, particularly crime statistics, generally improve as the population ages.

Simpson's Paradox

A common manifestation of a spurious relationship is the phenomenon of Simpson's paradox. Simpson's paradox occurs when a relationship that exists for all subgroups of a population disappears when the data are aggregated for the whole population (or the reverse in the case where there is no relationship among the subgroups). Gerald Bracey illustrated the paradox at work in the case of SAT verbal scores:[12] Critics of American education who cite the national average scores, Bracey argues, unfairly claim that there has been no improvement over two decades. The average verbal score for 2002 was unchanged from the score twenty-one years earlier (table 3.2), yet every subgroup of students taking the test recorded an increase in their scores.

How is it possible that all the ethnic groups have done better, but the country as a whole has not improved at all? Look closely at the data in

TABLE 3.2
SAT Verbal Scores, by Race and Ethnicity

	1981	2002	Gain
White	519	527	+8
Puerto Rican	437	455	+18
Mexican	438	446	+8
Black	412	431	+19
Asian	474	501	+27
American Indian	471	479	+8
All Students	504	504	0

Source: Gerald Bracey "Those Misleading SAT and NAEP Trends"

table 3.2 and see that white students are the only group above average in either year. White students comprised 85 percent of the test takers in 1981, but only 65 percent of the test takers in 2002.

Regression Fallacy

Over lunch in the faculty lounge, sociology professor Rumtoast[13] explained to me his philosophy of teaching and his strategy for motivating students to do well in his courses: Grade the students very hard on the first test. Rumtoast devised this strategy after observing a very common education-testing phenomenon: Students who did well on his midterms tended to get lower grades on the final exam, while students who did poorly at first tended to raise their scores on the final. The low scores on the first test, he explained, encouraged those students to study harder for the second exam, while those who received high scores were less motivated. Give all the students low scores, he reasoned, and they will all work harder.

I explained to Rumtoast that his analysis involved a regression fallacy (also known as a "regression to the mean" or "regression artifact") and that instead of worrying about motivating his students he ought to design some better tests.

To understand the problem with Professor Rumtoast's analysis, consider the experiment where I teach my students how to flip a coin so that it will be more likely to come up heads.

First I do a pretest: Each student in the class is instructed to flip a coin nine times and count the number of times it comes up heads. Those students with five or more heads are already doing well, so they will become the control group. Those who failed to get heads at least half of the time

Table 3.3
Results of Coin Flipping Experiment

Pretest Group (/9 flips):	% Heads		Net Change
	Pretest	Post-test	
More than 5 heads	63%	50%	-12.5
Less than 5 heads	37	50	+12.5

are assigned to the treatment group and are sent to another room and instructed to place their coins against their foreheads and repeat the phrase "Heads up" fifteen times. Properly trained, they return to class, where each student flips their coin nine more times for the posttest.

The results are inevitably as shown in table 3.3. The students who held the coin to their foreheads improved their coin-flipping by over 12 percent, while those who had done well at first (presumably because they were less motivated), saw their test scores go down.

Now imagine that half of Rumtoast's test was based on essay questions that everyone got right. The other half was based on true/false questions that no one knew the answer to. The students, in effect, flipped a coin.

Regression fallacies occur when subjects of an experiment are selected for their extreme scores on a "before" measure or when a policy is implemented in response to an unusually high or low score on a critical indicator. Bogus medical treatments often owe their popularity to regression artifacts. Many medical conditions (for example, arthritis) get better, then worse, and then better over time. The condition gets treated when it is at its worst and credit for the improvement is ascribed to the treatment. For centuries, doctors practiced bloodletting based on just such evidence.

Unfortunately, many government policies are evaluated based on the same kind of evidence: The crime rate spikes, and a new police chief is elected who experiments with a new policing strategy. The crime rate goes back down (it regresses back to the average, or the mean), and the police chief takes credit. Unemployment goes up; the incumbents are thrown out of office, and the new party takes credit when things improve. Although President Obama (at the end of 2011) seems to be an exception, the most successful presidents are usually those who have the good fortune to take office during hard economic times.

Instrumentation/Measurement Reliability

As noted in chapter 1, inconsistent and unreliable measures of the effect of a policy change can lead to faulty conclusions about the policy's effectiveness.

In 2009, Atlanta public school superintendent Beverly Hall received the U.S. Superintendent of the Year award based largely on her record of steadily improving scores on the tests mandated by the No Child Left Behind Act. In her first ten years as superintendent, she received over half a million dollars in salary bonuses based largely on the students' improved performance.[14] Hall retired just before a state panel investigating the test scores at fifty-six Atlanta schools found that 178 teachers and administrators at forty-four Atlanta public schools were caught cheating on the tests by erasing and changing the students' incorrect answers.[15] As we will see in the next chapter, similar investigations have questioned the validity of crime rate data.

Ecological Fallacy

Drawing an erroneous inference about individual behavior from a relationship based on aggregated geographical data can lead to an "ecological fallacy." Sociologist William S. Robinson coined the term in a 1950 article in which he observed that states with the highest rates of foreign-born population also had the highest literacy rates, even though the foreign-born population had lower literacy rates than the native-born population.[16]

Figure 3.3 depicts the relationship between the state vote for William Jennings Bryan in the 1900 presidential election and the percentage of each state's population that was black. There is clearly a strong positive relationship: The greater the black population in a state, the greater the share of the

Figure 3.3. State Vote for William Jennings Bryan and % Black, 1900.

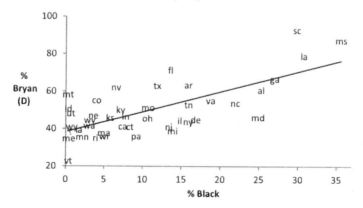

Sources: Census Bureau, Historical Census Statistics; Atlas of U.S. Presidential Elections.

vote for Bryan, the Democrat. Nevertheless, it would be an ecological fallacy to conclude that blacks were more likely to vote for Bryan than McKinley. From the time of the Civil War until the 1950s, most blacks who could vote voted Republican, the party of Lincoln.

There is an underlying causal relationship here: In those states with the largest black population, the white Democratic Party was the strongest and blacks were least likely to be able to vote at all.

The "Closing the Gap" Paradox

Really good news about the release of new statistical data often comes in the form of a finding that a disadvantaged group or a low-performing city, school district, or country is "closing the gap" with a comparison group or jurisdiction.[17] Under certain conditions, however, the finding, or more precisely, the conclusion drawn from the finding, is a statistical fallacy. The closing the gap fallacy occurs when:

- Both the higher- and lower-performing comparison groups have increased over time, with the lower-scoring groups increasing at a faster rate.
- The statistical indicator used is a percentage measure or has an upper limit (for example, a test score with a maximum score of 100 percent).
- The explanation given for the finding is that something was done to improve the score of the lower-performing group.

On May 13, 2009, a *Wall Street Journal* article announced, "Housing Boom Aided Minorities: Homeownership Reached Record Levels, Narrowing the Gap with Whites."[18] The evidence offered was that between 1995 and 2008, white homeownership rates increased by 6 percent, while black, Asian, and Hispanic homeownership rates increased by at least twice that rate (table 3.4a).

The paradox is that, if one takes the inverse of such data, the opposite conclusion is just as valid. The conclusion stated in the headline is correct, in a sense, but based on the data offered in the article, the headline could just as accurately have been, "Housing Boom Benefits Asians and Whites."

If we take the inverse of the homeownership data to measure the non-homeownership rates, we see (also in table 3.4a) that there was a greater decline in whites' non-homeownership than there was for blacks or Hispanics. So what we have here is two diametrically opposite conclusions drawn from the same data, both of which are correct. This is a paradox: seemingly contradictory findings that are both in a sense true.

TABLE 3.4a
Homeownership Rate, by Race and Ethnicity

	Homeownership rates		
	1995	2008	% Change
Black	42	48	13%
Hispanic	42	49	17%
Asian	49	59	20%
White	71	75	6%
	Home non-ownership rates		
Black	58	53	-9%
Hispanic	58	51	-12%
Asian	51	41	-20%
White	30	25	-15%

Source: *Wall Street Journal* 5/13/09

The paradox becomes a fallacy when the data lead to an incorrect causal conclusion. Here, the fallacy is not in the *Journal*'s headline but in the causal inference in the rest of the article, which seeks to explain why the minority homeownership gap was closed. The *Journal* explains: "During the same time period, blacks and Latinos were far more likely than whites to take out so-called subprime loans—those designed for people with weak credit records or high debt in relation to income." This is true, but blacks and Latinos who did not own homes did not benefit disproportionately from the housing boom; Asian and white non-homeowners did.

To convince yourself of this, imagine that in 1995 some new policy was implemented that randomly gave new homes to half of all the families who did not own homes. The policy would affect all non-homeowners equally, but those groups with the lowest rates of homeownership would close the gap in their homeownership rates (table 3.4b).

The lesson to be drawn from this is that conclusions about closing gaps are best drawn from comparisons of decreasing rates. Fortunately, most indicators with an upper limit score are such that one can fairly easily calculate the inverse score.

The Problem with Experiments: External Validity

Most causal fallacies could be avoided with a simple experimental design: Randomly assign subjects to treatment and control groups, apply an experimental treatment, and measure the effect. Assuming that enough subjects

TABLE 3.4b
Effect of Giving Homes to Half of all Non-homeowners

	Homeownership rates		
	1995	2008	% Change
Black	42	71	+69%
Hispanic	42	71	+69%
Asian	50	75	+50%
White	70	85	+21%
	Home non-ownership rates		
Black	58	29	-50%
Hispanic	58	29	-50%
Asian	50	25	-50%
White	30	15	-50%

are included in the experiment so the different outcomes are not due to chance (that is, sampling error) and that the control group is not exposed to some form of the treatment, the measured results must have been caused by the treatment.

On some occasions, policy researchers have been able to conduct random assignment experiments on public policy topics. One such experiment was conducted in 1974 by psychologist John Voevodsky, to test the effectiveness of Center High-Mounted Stop Lamps, or CHMSLs, the brake lights that are now mounted in the rear window of all U.S. passenger cars.[19]

Voevodsky conducted his experiment in San Francisco with taxicabs. The brake lights were installed on 343 randomly selected taxis, and 160 taxis were assigned to the control group, which had no third brake light. The results were quite dramatic: The taxis with the lights had more than 60 percent fewer rear-end collisions, 60 percent fewer injuries, and 60 percent lower repair costs. After larger experiments with Washington taxicabs and with telephone-company cars in four regions, which found similar results, the National Highway Traffic Safety Administration (NHTSA) mandated that CHMSLs be installed on all passenger cars in 1986.

A later NHTSA study measured the effects of CHMSLs after the lights were mandated over a period from 1986 to 1995, using accident data for cars with the new lights installed.[20] Once the lights were installed on most cars, rear-end crashes did decline, but only by 5 percent, not by the 60 percent that the experiment predicted, and the reductions were greatest in the earliest years of the study.

For the most part the initial experiments were entirely valid. In all likelihood, anyone who installed the lights in their cars in the 1970s probably would reduce their chances of a rear-end crash by 60 percent. The problem is that the experimental conditions did not match what would happen in the real world once the new policy was put into effect. The lights were new and very few people had ever seen them before. Once the lights were installed on most cars, people stopped paying attention.

The public school choice experiments often involve a potential threat to external validity. Many of the experimental results are based on comparisons of students in newly created schools with control group students in existing schools. Whatever the beneficial effect of the charter school instruction, it may be diminished by the fact these these are newly established schools. The principals are initially unfamiliar with the teachers, the students are going through the turmoil of enrolling in a new school, and few of the students' families are familiar with the administration. All these conditions make it difficult to generalize from the experimental setting to conclusions about the long-term benefits of the schools.

The problem of external validity concerns generalizing from experimental treatments and subjects to the real world and is most common in cancer experiments with laboratory rats. For the most part, such studies are internally valid (we don't let the rats self-select for their inclusion in the control group). But rats aren't people, and often the treatments in such experiments (exposures to high doses of potential carcinogens) do not correspond to human consumption patterns.

Notes

1. Donald T. Campbell and H. Laurence Ross, "The Connecticut Crackdown on Speeding: Time-Series Data in Quasi-Experimental Analysis," *Law & Society Review* 3, no. 33 (1968); H. L. Ross, Donald T. Campbell, and Gene V. Glass, "Determining the Social Effects of a Legal Reform: The British 'Breathalyser' Crackdown of 1967," *American Behavioral Scientist* 13, no. 4 (March 1970): 493–509.

2. "Global Warming Has Slowed Down over the Past 10 Years, Say Scientists," *Daily Mail*, November 23, 2010, at http://www.dailymail.co.uk/sciencetech/article-1333225/Global-warming-slowing-say-scientists.html.

3. John M. Broder, "Past Decade Warmest on Record, NASA Data Shows," *New York Times*, January 21, 2010, at http://www.nytimes.com/2010/01/22/science/earth/22warming.html.

4. Tax Foundation, "U.S. Federal Individual Income Tax Rates History, 1913–2007," February 27, 2007, at http://www.taxfoundation.org/taxdata/show/151.html.

5. Daniel J. Mitchell, "The Historical Lessons of Lower Tax Rates," Heritage Foundation, August 13, 2003, at http://www.heritage.org/Research/Taxes/wm327.cfm.

6. Daniel J. Mitchell, "Fifteen Reasons Why the Clinton Tax Package Would Be Bad for America's Future," Heritage Foundation, August 5, 1993, at http://www.heritage.org/Research/Reports/1993/08/Fifteen-Reasons-Why-the-Clinton -Tax-Package-Would-Be-Bad-for-Americas-Future.

7. V. O. Key Jr., *Southern Politics in State and Nation* (New York: Knopf, 1949).

8. Scott Gottlieb, "Medicaid Is Worse Than No Coverage at All," *Wall Street Journal*, March 10, 2011, at http://online.wsj.com/article/SB1000142405274870475890457618 82 80858303612.html.

9. Damien J. LaPar et al., "Primary Payer Status Affects Mortality for Major Surgical Operations," *Annals of Surgery* 252, no. 3 (September 2010): 544–51, at http://www.ncbi .nlm.nih.gov/pmc/articles/PMC3071622/table/T5/.

10. Amy Finkelstein, Sarah Taubman, Bill Wright, et al., "The Oregon Health Insurance Experiment: Evidence from the First Year," National Bureau of Economic Research, working paper 17190, July 2011, at http://www.nber.org/papers/w17190.

11. Finkelstein et al., "The Oregon Health Insurance Experiment," ii.

12. Gerald Bracey, "Those Misleading SAT and NAEP Trends: Simpson's Paradox at Work," Education Disinformation Detection and Reporting Agency, posted January 8, 2003, at http://www.america-tomorrow.com/bracey/EDDRA/EDDRA30.htm.

13. Not his real name (but he is a sociologist).

14. Ross McLaughlin, "Beverly Hall's Compensation Eclipsed Other Area Superintendents," 11Alive Center for Investigative Action, July 26, 2011, at http://www.11alive.com/rss/article/198910/3/Beverly-Halls-compensation-eclipsed-other-area-superintendents.

15. Robert E. Wilson, Michael J. Bowers, and Richard L. Hyde, "[Untitled] Report of the Governor's Special Investigators," June 30, 2011, at http://clatl.com/images/other/aps/vol1.pdf.

16. William S. Robinson, "Ecological Correlations and the Behavior of Individuals," *American Sociological Review* 15 (June 1950): 351–57.

17. Stephen Gorard comes close to describing the closing the gap fallacy, referring to it as the "politicians' error," in "Keeping a Sense of Proportion: The 'Politicians' Error' in Analysing School Outcomes," *British Journal of Educational Studies* 47, no. 3 (September 1999): 235–46. Gorard, however, does not recognize the simple solution of calculating the inverse and comparing rates in decline.

18. Miriam Jordan, "Housing Boom Aided Minorities, Homeownership Reached Record Levels, Narrowing the Gap with Whites," *Wall Street Journal*, May 13, 2009, at http://online.wsj.com/article/SB124214925172111415.html.

19. John Voevodsky, "Evaluation of a Deceleration Warning Light for Reducing Rear-End Automobile Collisions," *Journal of Applied Psychology* 59 (1974): 270–73.

20. Charles J. Kahane and Ellen Hertz, "The Long-Term Effectiveness of Center High Mounted Stop Lamps in Passenger Cars and Light Trucks," NHTSA Technical Report Number DOT HS 808 696, March 1998, at http://www.nhtsa.gov/cars/rules/regrev/evaluate/808696.html.

CHAPTER 4

Examining a Relationship
New York City Crime Rates

THROUGHOUT the 2008 presidential campaign, Republican candidate Rudy Giuliani highlighted his accomplishments as mayor of New
York City, particularly his record in reducing the city's crime rate. When
he became mayor in 1994, New York City had endured three decades of
decline, riots, decaying infrastructure, rising crime, police corruption, and
racial and ethnic turmoil. A former successful federal prosecutor, Giuliani
entered office on a law-and-order platform; by the time he left office, shortly
after the 9/11 tragedy, the city had undergone a remarkable transformation.
A news account in *The Economist* summarizes the record: "Crime halved
under Mr. Giuliani and murders fell by two-thirds, transforming New York
from one of the most dangerous cities in America to one of the safest."[1]

The crime reductions were significant not only in terms of the support they
lent to the Giuliani campaign, but also because they are often cited as evidence
of the success of a dramatic and controversial strategy of policing large cities.
Soon after Giuliani became mayor in January of 1994, he appointed William
J. Bratton as police commissioner. Bratton initiated a new policing strategy
involving the use of CompStat, a new computerized system for tracking and
responding to changes in neighborhood crime. He instituted a crackdown on
less serious crimes (such as graffiti and subway turnstile jumping) and began
the use of "stop and frisk" searches for illegal handguns. (Giuliani did not often
mention his enforcement of the strict New York City gun laws during the campaign.) There were new restrictions on the homeless and a variety of other
aggressive policing measures that drove civil libertarians to outrage.

Few contest that there were substantial reductions in crime over
the course of the Giuliani administration, and the FBI Uniform Crime
Report data (table 4.1) indicate that *The Economist* accurately summarized
Giuliani's record. Violent crimes *were* cut in half, and murders *did* fall by
almost two-thirds.

51

TABLE 4.1
New York City Crime Counts, 1993 and 2001 (thousands)

	1993	2001	Net Change	% Change
Murder\manslaughter	1.9	0.7	-1.2	-63%
Rape	2.8	1.7	-1.2	-41%
Robbery	86.0	30.5	-55	-65%
Aggravated assault	62.8	41.5	-21	-34%
Violent crimes	**153.5**	**74.4**	**-79**	**-52%**
Burglary	99.2	34.4	-65	-65%
Larceny-theft	235.1	146.1	-89	-38%
Motor vehicle theft	112.5	32.6	-80	-71%
Property crimes	**446.8**	**213.2**	**-234**	**-52%**

Source: FBI Uniform Crime Report

Nevertheless, Giuliani's critics dispute the claim that the mayor and his policies were responsible for the reductions. Giuliani biographer Wayne Barrett argues that the decline in the crime rates began under the previous mayor, David Dinkins, and that the reason for the decline had more to do with general national economic prosperity of the 1990s, which led crime rates to fall in other cities at the same time. Steven D. Levitt and Stephen J. Dubner, authors of *Freakonomics*,[2] also credit Dinkins for initiating a police department hiring binge that, they calculate, accounts for all of New York's above-average crime reduction. Levitt and Dubner also suggest that Police Commissioner Bratton deserves more credit than Giuliani. Bratton was fired two years into his term, allegedly for taking too much credit and shortly after his picture appeared on the cover of *Time* magazine.[3]

The dispute over who deserves credit for the drop in crime is somewhat beside the point if there really was no significant reduction. On this point, Barrett insists that the Giuliani administration manipulated the crime statistics: "Rudy Giuliani is not a management expert, he is a statistical expert. He has jimmied every number we live by."[4] Most of the crime reduction, Barrett adds, was for nonviolent crimes such as larcenies under $50 (15 percent of the reduction) and auto and auto-parts theft (42 percent of the reduction).

Lastly, Levitt and Dubner and, in a separate study, Rick Nevin, have offered two intriguing alternative explanations for the decline in New York's crime rates, having to do with abortion and lead-eradication policy changes that occurred decades before Giuliani took office.

To evaluate the merits of the Giuliani claim, it is necessary to address the possible statistical fallacies and alternative explanations for the drop in crime in light of additional evidence. The possibilities include:

a. *A regression artifact*: Giuliani may have taken office at a time when crime rates were at an unusual peak.
b. *Maturation and long-term processes*: Barrett's claim that rates fell in other cities at the same time suggests that a general national economic or maturation effect might account for the drop. This would include the aging of the population (most violent crimes are committed by young males) and the stabilization of the crack cocaine epidemic.
c. *Historical events*: Here we have the possibilities that Dinkins, the hiring binge he initiated, or Bratton was more responsible for the reductions.
d. *Instrumentation*: This would involve Barrett's allegation that the crime statistics were manipulated.
e. *Other causes*: This will include that possibility that New York City particularly benefited from policy changes in the 1970s concerning abortion and lead eradication.

We can begin by dismissing Barrett's claim that most of the crime reduction was for minor crimes. It's true, and it fits with the NYPD strategy of targeting minor crimes, but this is nothing more than cherry picking on Barrett's part: Both violent and nonviolent crime fell at the same rate.

To assess the other counterarguments, consider first the data shown in figure 4.1, depicting the trend in New York City's crime rate against the backdrop of the crime rates in the sixty-six largest cities (for an explanation of the boxplots, see chapter 6). The data indicate that some of New York's crime drop can be explained by whatever caused crime to drop in almost every other large city at the same time, although New York clearly outperformed those cities. New York's crime rate was in the top quartile of large cities in 1994 (New York ranked 10th) and fell below the median (ranking 35th) in 2002, the year Giuliani left office. And crime continued to fall after Giuliani left office; by 2009 three-fourths of the large cities had higher violent crime rates (New York ranking 48th).

There is no evidence here of a regression artifact. The year 1993 was not an unusually high-crime year, but Barrett and Levitt and Dubner are correct in noting that crime did start to fall during Dinkins's administration. Moreover, it would be unfair not to give Dinkins some credit for the 10 percent reduction in violent crime rates in the year after he left office, or Giuliani for the 7 percent drop the year after he left office.[5]

Figure 4.1. Violent Crime Rates (per 100,000 population): New York City (line) and 66 Largest Cities (cities with population >250,000) (boxplot).

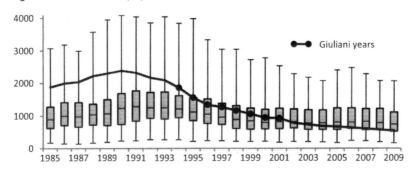

Source: FBI Uniform Crime Report.

The crime data depicted in table 4.1 and figure 4.1 are derived from the FBI Uniform Crime Report based on NYPD reporting and, after 1994, NYPD's CompStat reports. The allegation of data manipulation is based on the idea that, once CompStat was implemented, police commanders were held accountable for their precinct's crime rates and had an incentive and opportunity to underreport crimes, particularly crimes such as aggravated assault, where the classification of the crime is a matter of subjective judgment.

Most recently, some evidence has come to light to support Barrett's claim. A survey of precinct managers by John A. Eterno and Eli B. Silverman found that managers felt they were subject to substantial pressure during the CompStat era to underreport crime, and many of the managers were aware of instances where "ethically inappropriate" changes were made in crime classifications.[6] In the fall of 2010, the new police commissioner appointed a panel to conduct an investigation into the city's crime-reporting practices after officers in one Brooklyn precinct were charged with failing to report felony incidents.[7]

Although the total violent crime rate is the most comprehensive measure of how safe cities are, the murder rate is a more reliable measure: There may be murders that go undetected, but it is highly unlikely that any general police practice would result in deliberate underreporting of murders. And for the most part, the murder rate data (figure 4.2) lend stronger support to the Giuliani thesis: the murder rate drop is steeper (66 percent vs. 53 percent) and there is a sharper break between the Giuliani and Dinkins years. Nevertheless, there is good reason to give Dinkins credit for at least some of the 1994 drop.

In addition to the murder rate data, some National Criminal Victimization Survey (NCVS) data for the first six years of Giuliani's term have been provided by two Bureau of Justice Statistics researchers, Patrick Langan and

Figure 4.2. New York City Murder Rate (per 100,000 population).

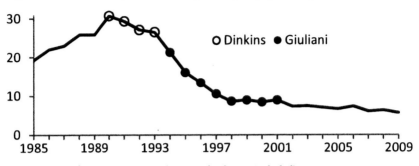

Source: FBI Uniform Crime Report (9/11/01 deaths not included).

Matthew Durose.[8] The NCVS data, derived from a household survey completely independent of police department reporting, differ in some ways from the FBI data. The NCVS records crimes committed against New York residents over twelve years of age, while the police department data include commercial crimes and crimes committed against youths and nonresidents. Nevertheless, the NCVS data indicate a slightly larger drop in the violent crime rate for New York City than do the FBI data collected by the NYPD (table 4.2).

Langan and Durose took their investigation a step further by investigating the reliability of New York City's murder statistics, comparing them to the city medical examiner's homicide records, and found that murder had been underreported in the city. In 1999, for example, the medical examiner reported nineteen homicides that were not recorded by the NYPD and reported to the FBI. Nevertheless, there were fewer of these nonreported homicides under Giuliani than there were under Dinkins. In 1993, the NYPD had reported fifty-five fewer homicides than the medical examiner.[9] In general, the alternative measures corroborate the FBI and CompStat data.

Levitt and Dubner (like Barrett) argue that Dinkins deserves some of the credit for hiring more police officers, although, they say, he did so only after he knew Giuliani would be his chief opponent. Between 1991 and 2001, they say, the NYPD went through a "hiring binge" and the "NYPD grew by 45 percent, more than three times the national average."[10] Using some calculation that they do not explain, they estimate that the increased police hiring alone "would be expected to reduce crime in New York by 18 percent relative to the national average," and thus account for all of the city's above-average reduction in crime.

The *Freakonomics* data are correct; there were 13,000 more full-time officers on the NYPD rolls by 2001, but an instrumentation problem clouds their data. The rolls did increase every year Dinkins was in office (well

TABLE 4.2
Percent Change in Violent Crime Rates, 1993-1999

	New York City	National
Violent Crime (FBI)	-49%	-30%
Murder rate (FBI)	-66*	-40
Violent Crime (NCVS)	-53*	-34

Sources: FBI; Bureau of Justice Statistics; *Langan and Durose

before Giuliani became a candidate), but most of the increase happened in 1995, the year the city added its Transit Authority and Public Housing Authority officers to the NYPD ranks. Between 1995 and 2002, the NYPD actually lost more than two hundred officers (figure 4.3), while the city's violent crime rank fell from 18 to 36.

That leaves Barrett's claim that the drop in crime that was not due to statistical manipulation was actually a result of the city's economic prosperity. Most researchers acknowledge that the overall drop in the nation's crime rate in the 1990s was due in large part to the economic growth of the time (following the Clinton tax increases in 1993), and the unusually good economic prosperity that New York City enjoyed in the 1990s may account for its success in reducing crime.

Separating out the effect of two simultaneous causes—the impact of the economy from the impact of Giuliani administration policies—would take a really complicated form of non–plain data analysis and might be beside the point, as Giuliani also takes credit for the city's economic prosperity during his administration.

To test this alternative, we can compare the ratio of the city's murder rate to the national rate to the ratio of the city's unemployment rate to the

Figure 4.3. New York City Police Department: Full-Time Officers.

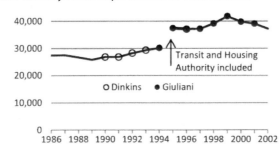

Source: Langan and Durose.

national rate (figure 4.4). New York City's murder rate peaked at over three times the national rate in 1989 (Dinkins's first year in office); the unemployment rate peaked at twice the national average in 1997. Note that the murder rate ratio fell for eight consecutive years before the unemployment rate ratio started to go down.

It may be true that New York City's crime rates would not have fallen as far as they did had it not been for the city's economic performance, but the evidence is stronger that the economy would not have done as well as it did had it not been for the drop in the crime rate.

Levitt and Dubner's most controversial argument is that New York State's legalization of abortion in 1970—three years before *Roe v. Wade*—resulted in the city's crime rate falling earlier than in the rest of the country. Fewer unwanted children were born in New York in the early 1970s, they reason; in other states those unwanted children would have been more likely to grow up to be criminals. Their evidence is based on a comparison of the crime rates in early- and late-legalizing states: "Between 1988 and 1994 violent crime in the early-legalizing states fell 13 percent compared to the other states; between 1994 and 1997, their murder rates fell 23 percent more than those of the other states."[11]

Comparing the change in murder rates in those cities where abortion was legalized early (table 4.3), provides some interesting confirmation of Levitt and Dubner's argument: Of the large cities in early-legalization states, murder rates fell by 53 percent during Giuliani's term and only 33 percent in the other cities. The murder rate fell faster in New York City and all but three of these cities, but the reduction was only 10 percent greater than the early-legalization city average. (Note: "city average" is the average of the city rates and is not weighted for the city's population.) Most intriguing, however, is what happened after Giuliani left office. New York City continued

Figure 4.4. New York City Murder and Unemployment Rates: Ratios to National Rates.

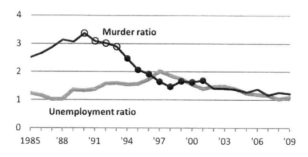

Sources: FBI Uniform Crime Report; Bureau of Labor Statistics.

TABLE 4.3
Change in Murder Rates in Large Early-Abortion-Legalization*
Cities, 1993 - 2001

	1993	2001	% change	2009	% change 2001-09
Anaheim	11.9	2.4	-80%	2.7	+13%
Santa Ana	26.8	7.0	-74%	7.4	+6%
New York City	**26.5**	**8.9**	**-66%**	**5.6**	**-37%**
San Diego	11.5	4.0	-65%	3.1	-23%
Seattle	12.6	4.4	-65%	3.7	-16%
Long Beach	28.4	10.4	-63%	8.6	-17%
Fresno	22.9	9.2	-60%	8.7	-5%
Anchorage	9.2	3.8	-59%	4.9	+29%
Sacramento	22.0	9.6	-56%	6.4	-33%
San Francisco**	17.5	8.0	-54%	5.6	-30%
San Jose	5.1	2.4	-53%	2.9	+21%
Oakland	40.8	20.6	-50%	25.7	+25%
Los Angeles	30.5	15.6	-49%	8.1	-48%
Riverside	13.7	7.7	-44%	5.0	-35%
Stockton	20.3	12.1	-40%	11.3	-7%
Bakersfield	14.2	8.7	-39%	8.2	-6%
Honolulu	3.5	2.3	-34%	1.5	-35%
Buffalo	23.4	21.8	-7%	22.3	+2%
city averages:					
early-adopters	18.9	8.8	-53%	7.9	-11%
late-adopters	20.1	13.4	-33%	11.3	-16%

*early adoption states: (two years before Roe v. Wade) New York, California, Washington, Alaska and Hawaii
**San Francisco's 2001 rate is the average of its 2000 and 2002 rates
Source: FBI Uniform Crime Report

to reduce its murder rate at an impressive rate; only one city did better after 2001. After 2001, the early-legalization cities lost ground. This is probably what one would expect from the abortion-crime hypothesis: Over the long term, the late-legalization cities caught up.

One last telling fact reveals itself in the post-2001 data. Of all the late-adoption cities, the one with the biggest murder rate reduction is Los Angeles (and this is true of the violent crime rate as well). In 2002, William Bratton was appointed the Los Angeles chief of police.

Other, largely nonquantifiable factors peculiar to the times and the city may have been at work. Among the more intriguing explanations is that the decline in children's exposure to lead, beginning in the 1970s, accounted for the national reduction in crime in the 1990s. Economist Rick Nevin's research, for example, identifies a strong link between children's exposure to lead and crime rate trends across nine nations and in U.S. cities.[12] Reduced child lead exposure, he argues, means fewer children suffering from the mental impairments that lead to criminality. He also disputes Levitt's abortion crime explanation, noting that California's restrictions on leaded gasoline, enacted in 1978, five years before the U.S. restrictions, presaged its early drop in crime. New York City banned lead paint in 1960, eighteen years before the U.S. ban took effect (and fifty years after the French, Belgian, and Austrian bans on indoor lead paint), and the city began regulating lead emissions in the 1960s, policies that reduced child lead exposure to well below the national average. The regulations, Nevin argues, better account for the New York City crime drop and the persistence of high levels of crime in the rest of the state (see, for example, Buffalo in table 4.3).

In cities across America in the 1990s, mayors touted their success in fighting crime in their reelection campaigns. For most, it was dumb luck; they just happened to be in office at the right time. As for Giuliani, the evidence presented here offers no final proof that the mayor's policies reduced crime, but most of the counterarguments, with the exception of Nevin's lead paint hypothesis, do not hold up.

NOTES

1. "From America's Mayor to America's President?" *The Economist,* May 3, 2007, at http://www.economist.com/world/na/displaystory.cfm?story_id=9119759.

2. Steven D. Levitt and Stephen J. Dubner, *Freakonomics: A Rogue Economist Explores the Hidden Side of Everything* (New York: William Morrow, 2004).

3. "Finally, We're Winning the War against Crime," *Time,* January 15, 1996.

4. Wayne Barrett, "Giuliani's Legacy: Taking Credit for Things He Didn't Do," *Gotham Gazette,* June 25, 2001, at http://www.gothamgazette.com/commentary/91.barrett.shtml.

5. None of the New York City 2001 homicide figures include the 2,823 persons killed at the World Trade Center on September 11.

6. John A. Eterno and Eli B. Silverman, "NYPD's Compstat: Compare Statistics or Compose Statistics?" *International Journal of Police Science and Management* 12, no. 3 (2010): 426–49; see also John Eck and Edward Maguire, "Have Changes in Policing Reduced Violent Crime? An Assessment of the Evidence," in *The Crime Drop in America,* edited by Alfred Blumstein and Joel Wallman, 207–65 (Cambridge, UK: Cambridge University Press, 2000).

7. Al Baker and William K. Rashbaum, "New York City to Examine Reliability of Its Crime Reports," *New York Times*, January 6, 2011.

8. Patrick A. Langan and Matthew R. Durose, "The Remarkable Drop in Crime in New York City," paper presented at the International Conference on Crime, Rome, Italy, December 2003, at http://www.istat.it/istat/eventi/2003/perunasocieta/relazioni/Langan_rel.pdf.

9. Langan and Durose, "The Remarkable Drop," table 1.

10. Levitt and Dubner, *Freakonomics*, 129.

11. Levitt and Dubner, *Freakonomics*, 140.

12. Rick Nevin, "Understanding International Crime Trends: The Legacy of Preschool Lead Exposure," *Environmental Research* 104, no. 3 (July 2007): 315–36.

CHAPTER 5

Tabulating the Data and Writing about the Numbers

Getting information from a table is like extracting sunbeams from a cucumber.
—ARTHUR BRIGGS FARQUHAR AND HARRY FARQUHAR[1]

RESEARCH REPORTS and analyses based on numerical information should accommodate two different audiences: those who read the text but ignore the data presented in tables and charts, and those who skim the text and grasp the main ideas from the data presentation. To serve the latter audience, tables (and charts, discussed in the next chapter) should be self-explanatory, conveying the critical ideas contained in the data without relying on the text to explain what the numbers mean. The text should accommodate readers who skim past the numbers, providing a general summary of the most important ideas illustrated by the data—without repeating many of the numbers contained in the tables. When done well, tables will complement the text and permit careful readers to critically evaluate the evidence for the conclusions presented in the text.

Combining tabulated data with a textual summary can provide for an effective presentation of information. A comprehensive and detailed tabulation is open to the reader's interpretation of the key numerical comparisons and insights, while a concise textual summary exerts the author's control over the information. Consider, for example, a newspaper story about a baseball game accompanied by a standard game box score. The story tells of the key plays and events of the game, perhaps with a focus on the home team, and highlights some of the statistical information in the box score. For a real baseball fan who knows the difference between GIDP, ERA, and HBP, a box score tells the whole story and in just a few minutes conveys more information about the game than a whole page of the sports section could.

The critical difference between a baseball-story-and-box-score and a research report containing a textual discussion of tabulated data is that a box score does not allow for any unique authorship; the content is defined by a predetermined format. The box score will be the same in the hometown and visiting newspapers. When presenting data in a research report or analytical essay, the author has much more control over the content and organization of the data. Most of the social indicator data that are available come in a variety of formats involving choices of selecting a time frame and whether to use numerical counts, per capita, per GDP, rates and ratios, or measures of dispersion. The author has choices about how to format a table in order to make an effective presentation.

Three general principles guide the selection and presentation of numerical data: The text and/or the tabulation should contain meaningful measures and comparisons; the data should be unambiguous; and the presentation should convey the most important ideas about the data efficiently.

Choosing Meaningful Measures and Making Meaningful Comparisons

Going from a Census Bureau tabulation containing hundreds of thousands of numbers related to a specific topic to a table containing just a few numbers relevant to the discussion in the text involves many choices. In selecting some data and not others and arranging the information in a specific way, the author makes choices to highlight some of the statistics and to ignore others, preferably in a manner that is most consistent with the discussion in the text.

Counts, Rates, and Measures of Dispersion

Numerical counts of social indicator data, such as the number of persons unemployed (approximately 25 million) or uninsured (50 million), and aggregate totals of budgetary data, such as the national debt ($14 trillion) or military spending ($550 billion), more often than not serve as attention-getting or headline-grabbing numbers rather than as the basis for meaningful analysis. Most readers would be just as shocked by a headline that says "U.S. Debt Hits 14 Trillion" as they would by one that said "U.S. Debt Hits 14 Billion." For most purposes, but especially when making comparisons among groups and over time, rates and ratios are the more meaningful numbers to use.

TABLE 5.1a

Health Insurance Coverage, by Selected Characteristics, 2005 and 2010

	Number Uninsured*			% Uninsured*			% of uninsured
	2005	2010	% Change	2005	2010	Net Change	2010
Age	(millions)						
Under 18	7.6	7.3	-4	10.3	9.8	-.5	15
18 to 24	7.8	8.1	+4	28.0	27.2	-.8	16
25 to 34	9.8	11.8	+20	24.8	28.4	+3.6	24
35 to 44	7.6	8.7	+14	17.7	21.8	+4.1	17
45 to 54	6.0	7.9	+32	14.1	18.0	+3.9	16
55 to 64	3.7	5.3	+43	11.9	14.4	+2.5	11
65 and over	0.4	0.8	+87	1.2	2.0	+.8	2
Total	43.3	49.9	+15	14.6	16.3	+1.7	100
Work experience (age 18-64)							
Full-time	20.7	20.2	-3	17.2	17.5	+.3	48
Part-Time	5.5	7.8	+42	22.1	27.6	+5.5	19
Did Not work	10.0	13.8	+38	26.1	28.5	+2.4	33
Total	36.3	41.8	+15	19.7	21.8	+2.1	100
In Families below poverty	12.1	14.5	+20	30.4	31.4	+1.0	29

*uninsured for entire year

Source: Census Bureau, *Income, Poverty, and Health Insurance Coverage: 2010*

Table 5.1a reports uninsurance data using numerical counts, rates, and in the right-hand column, percentage distributions. A textual summary of the data might highlight some of the numerical counts: 50 million Americans went uninsured for the entire year in 2010, an increase of 3.6 million over five years. Twenty million Americans worked full-time (year round) yet had no insurance coverage. But for the most part, the counts in the table do not say much. Is the 15 million increase in the number uninsured due to a larger population? The numbers of uninsured for each age group, and the percentages of the uninsured in each age group, are particularly useless as they are not adjusted for the size of the age group or changes in the size of the age groups over time. As a general rule, rates and ratio (here, the % Uninsured) serve best for making comparisons across the demographic groups.

It is common to see tables containing two columns of distribution percentages, asking the reader to compare the distribution of a condition over demographic groups with the groups' percentages of the population, similar

Table 5.1b
Health Insurance Coverage, by Work
Experience, Age 18-64: 2010

	% of the uninsured	% of age 18-65
Full-time	48	60
Part-Time	19	15
Did Not work	33	25

to the two right-hand columns in table 5.1b. The conclusion would be that those who did not work are one-third of the uninsured, even though they make up only one-quarter of the working-age population. For what the author is trying to convey, the rate data (the left-hand column) suffice and convey the idea more efficiently.

Thus, the most meaningful comparisons in table 5.1 are based on the uninsurance rates. Here we see that younger persons, age 18 to 34, are the most likely to be uninsured. This is relevant to two key features of the "Obamacare" legislation: the requirement that insurance companies extend coverage under parents' insurance plans to dependent ("dependent" is a key word here) children until age 26, and the individual mandate that is intended to reduce insurance costs by requiring that younger, healthier workers enroll in the insurance plans.

Selecting a Time Frame

Depending on the data, the subject, and the purposes for which the data are used, longer time frames are generally preferable to shorter time frames. Each year the Illinois State Police prepare a 250-page Uniform Crime Report, containing the crime statistics for every county and police department in Illinois. The time frame for the great preponderance of the data in the report is the previous two years. The data in the report are commonly cited in local newspaper stories the day after the report's release. The data for one city, Normal, Illinois (yes, there is such a place), are shown in table 5.2. The complete tabulation is organized by county and permits comparisons between police departments within counties. Bloomington, Normal's twin city, had a slightly higher crime rate in 2009 (3,189).

The newspaper stories following the release of the Illinois report summarize the data for the counties and towns in their coverage area, but reporters do not go back to the stories they did one, two, or five years before to report on the long-term trend. The state police have copies of the same

TABLE 5.2

Illinois State Police Uniform Crime Report: Crime Index Offenses: Normal, Illinois Police Department, 2009

Year	Rate per 100,000	Total Crime Index Offenses	Murder	Criminal Sexual Assault	Robbery	Aggravated Assault/ Battery	Burglary	Theft	Motor Vehicle Theft	Arson
2009	3,008.3	1,566	0	29	24	126	364	992	24	7
2008	3,376.1	1,746	1	19	43	197	329	1,107	45	5
% Chg	-10.9%	-10.3%	-100%	52.6%	-44.2%	-36%	10.6%	-10.4%	-46.7%	40.0%

Source: Illinois State Police, *Crime in Illinois 2009*

report on their website going back to 1997, but the earlier data never made it into the annual report.[2] In general, an indicator such as a crime rate, particularly for a smaller city, bounces around; the long-term trend may be up or down, but a one-year change doesn't really tell much. As we saw with the crime rate data in the previous chapter, the change in any given year is unlikely to capture what is really going on. Over a five-year period, Normal's crime rate has gone down just 6 percent; and over a ten-year period, it is down 25 percent.

Measuring Change

In a table, change over time can be measured three different ways: net change, percentage change, and sometimes, the compounded annual rate of change.

In writing about changes in percentage rates, it is common that authors confuse, or leave ambiguous, net change, percentage change, and percentage point change. To say that unemployment has gone up 5 percent could mean that the number of unemployed persons has increased 5 percent (say, from 20 million to 21 million unemployed) or that the unemployment rate has gone up 5 percent (from 10 percent to 10.5 percent). As often as not, however, when people say the unemployment rate has gone up 5 percent, they really mean that it has gone up 5 percentage points (from 10 percent to 15 percent).

Presenting Data Unambiguously

Whether the information presented in a table is unambiguous depends largely on the descriptive text contained in the titles, headings, and notes. The table titles, column and row headings and subheadings, and footnotes should convey the general purpose of the table, explain coding, scaling, and definition of the variables, and define relevant terms or abbreviations.

Table 5.3 is an example of egregiously ambiguous data definition, which is evident if one tries to answer these questions: Does the birthrate measure the percentage of teenagers who give birth or the percentage of children born to teen mothers? Is the change the net change or the percentage change? Such ambiguities are even more common in written summaries of data than in tables.

The essential idea of a table is to facilitate numerical comparisons by organizing data into rows and columns. In the most common form of a table, the numbers are defined by the table title, column headings, row labels, and notes. Thus the title in table 5.4 indicates that all the numbers

TABLE 5.3

Change in Teenage Birth Rates: 1987-98

White	6.7%
Black	-4.9
Asian	-1.8
Hispanic	3.7

Source: US Statistical Abstract 2000, table 85

in the table are measures of the child poverty rate, which varies across and down the groups specified by the column and row headings. A spanning ("Head of Household") column heading defines similar columns. Because of the complicated categories of race and ethnicity used by the U.S. Census, annotations are used to define fully the row label categories.

The titles, headings, and notes should precisely define what each number in the table represents. When reporting rates or ratios, both the numerator and denominator should be clearly defined. Pay particular attention to whether the raw count numbers are reported in hundreds, thousands, or millions and whether monetary data are in current or constant (inflation-adjusted) dollars. The amount of detail given to defining the data depends on the audience. In a paper written for economists, it would not be necessary to define terms like GDP (gross domestic product), unemployment rate (the percentage of the labor force seeking work), or PPP (purchasing power parity); for other audiences more detail may need to be provided.

TABLE 5.4

Poverty Rate of Children by Family Status, Race, and Ethnicity, 2005

	Head of household			
	Married couple	Single male	Single female	All children
White*	8.0	17.5	38.7	10.0
Asian**	8.3	11.5	24.6	10.3
Black**	11.9	31.0	49.4	33.5
Hispanic	20.1	23.6	50.1	28.3
All races	8.5	19.9	42.6	17.6

*White alone, not Hispanic
**race alone or in combination (Hispanics of any race)
Source: Census Bureau, Annual Social and Economic Supplement, 2006 table POV01

Table Titles

A complete table (or chart) title fully defines the three components of the social indicator in the table: the count, the divisor, and the comparisons, as in the following examples:

- Public and Private Health Care Expenditures, OECD nations (% of GDP), 2010
- U.S. Public Health Care Expenditures, Per Capita: 1975–2004 (constant 1999 dollars)
- Murder Rates in Wealthy Nations: 1999 (homicides per 100,000 population)
- State Voter Turnout Rates, Presidential Elections: 1992–2004 (votes cast/voting age population)

In books, lengthy reports, and theses that contain an index of tables and figures, the titles should include more detail and often include information repeated in the row and column headings. In less formal writing, table titles sometimes state an explicit conclusion more forcefully. Thus, table 5.4 might be titled "Poverty Is Mostly a Function of Family Status, Not Race," with the actual definition of the variables reserved for subtitles and footnotes.

Almost all tables and charts covering a single year should have the year stated in the table title, and most multiyear tables should have the time range specified in the title.

Labeling the Rows and Columns

Column headings and row labels should be as brief and succinct as possible while still fully describing the data. Spanning headings and row-spanning row and column labels ("Head of Household" in table 5.4; "Work experience" in table 5.1a) are used to eliminate redundant text. Totals and summative measures are best placed on the right-hand columns and either at the top or bottom rows.

Sources

Fully specifying the sources of the data in the table lends authenticity to the numbers presented, expresses a willingness to allow readers to fact-check the data, and for readers familiar with different sources of similar data, aids in defining the data. Although nonacademic writing often contains sketchy and vague citations of data sources (such as "U.S. Census Bureau," or "World Bank"), such practices often indicate sloppy research and should be avoided. A fundamental principle of social science research is that the empirical findings should be replicable.[3] To this end, citations and data definitions should be sufficient to direct readers who would seek to confirm the accuracy of the data to the exact source of the data.

Unfortunately, for several reasons, this book does not follow its own advice: The sources at the bottom of the tables and charts generally only indicate the agency and publication of the data source. There are a couple of reasons for this. For some tables with several indicators from several sources (such as figure 1.1), a complete set of citations would take up more room than the table itself. In addition, almost all of the data were obtained on the Internet, and a complete citation should include the link to the site. A printed Internet link, however, can be several lines long, and asking researchers to retype a link that contains many random numbers is not very helpful. As an alternative, this book's companion website (http://pol.illinoisstate.edu/jpda/) will contain complete citations for each table and figure, including active hyperlinks to the data source (and to the actual spreadsheet files containing the tables and figures).

PRESENTING DATA EFFICIENTLY

There are two types of tables. Just about all of the numerical data included in this book were originally found in "look up" tables, databases, or spreadsheets compiled by government statistical agencies or nongovernmental organizations. The general and limited purpose of these tabulations is to present all the numerical information available that might be relevant to a wide variety of data users. For the most part, each table's text draws no conclusions about the data and serves only to describe how the data were obtained and to define what the numbers mean. The tables contained in analytical writing, however, serve a different purpose: the presentation of numerical evidence to support specific conclusions contained in the text. To serve this purpose, much care must be given to the design of the table.

An efficient tabular display will allow a reader to quickly discern the purpose and importance of the data and to draw a variety of interesting conclusions from a large amount of information. The measure of a table's efficiency is the number of meaningful comparisons that can readily be drawn from the data presentation. How quickly a reader can digest the information presented, discern the critical relationships among the data, and draw meaningful conclusions depends on how well the table is formatted.

Efficiency is often a matter of balance: More data allows for more comparison, but too much data can obscure meaningful comparison. A properly formatted table allows the reader to quickly draw the correct conclusion.

Organizing Rows and Columns

As a rule, similar data ought to be presented down the columns of the table. There are times when it can't be avoided, but mixing data of different types and measured on different scales in the same column can be disorienting. Table 5.5b is better than table 5.5a.

Sorting

The "look up" tables of most reference sources generally list data for geographic units (countries, states, or cities) alphabetically. If you are using a table to make a point, the reader will discern the point more quickly if the

TABLE 5.5a

Income, Poverty and Education, by Race and Hispanic Origin: 1998

	White	Asian*	Hispanic**	Black
Median Family Income	49,023	52,826	29,608	29,404
Poverty Rate	10.1	12.5	25.6	26.1
% High School Graduates	84.3	84.7	56.1	77.0

*Asian and Pacific Islander

**Hispanics many be of any race

Source: *Statistical Abstract*, 2000. Tables 737, 755, 250

TABLE 5.5b

Income, Poverty and Education, by Race and Hispanic Origin: 1998

	Median Family Income	Poverty Rate	% High School Graduates
White	49,023	10.1	84.3
Asian*	52,826	12.5	84.7
Hispanic**	29,608	25.6	56.1
Black	29,404	26.1	77.0

data are sorted on a meaningful variable. Although Cubs fans might find it inspiring (their team has only finished in first place nine times in the last hundred years), consider why baseball standings are not presented as they are in table 5.6.

The most common data tabulation mistake is to sort the data alphabetically. The alphabet is almost never the most meaningful variable. In his many books on effective data presentation, Howard Wainer, the most persistent critic of alphabetical sorting, decries table after table organized around the principle of "Alabama First!" and "Afghanistan First!"[4]

A properly sorted table will reveal things about the data that otherwise would remain hidden. Consider, for example, the advantage of table 5.7-B over the alphabetical sorting in table 5.7-A. See how much more quickly you can identify the countries where students watch the most and the least TV, the high-to-low variation in the data, and which country (Italy) is the median.

Decimal Places and Rounding

For most purposes, it is sufficient to limit the number of decimal places to two or three significant digits. It is usually not necessary to include dollar signs or percentage signs next to the numbers in a table, although this is sometimes done for the first number in a column. Large population counts and government expenditures should be listed in thousands, millions, or billions of dollars to retain two or three significant digits without using more than one decimal place.

Howard Wainer insists that there is no reason to display more than two significant digits in most tabular displays. He would eliminate the decimal points for the poverty and high school graduates data in table 5.5 and report the median family income in thousands of dollars, without decimal places.[5]

I think Wainer goes too far. Presumably, his rule would have Major League Baseball record the Cubs' winning percentage as "44 percent" rather than the .438 proportion. It is true that readers will look at the unrounded income data in table 5.5 and, in their minds, round off to thousands, and that the income data are based on estimates that make any conclusion based on differences of less than a thousand dollars practically meaningless. Nevertheless, the unrounded income figures will allow general readers, I think, to more quickly distinguish the income column from the percentage columns and to more easily discern that it is annual income that is being reported.

Although baseball statistics usually meet the highest standards for the display of data, it is odd that they report both the winning record and batting averages in proportions (.438) rather than percentages (43.8 percent).

TABLE 5.6
Final Major League Baseball Standings, 2011

National League Central	W	L	Pct	GB
Chicago Cubs	71	91	.438	25
Cincinnati Reds	79	83	.488	17
Houston Astros	56	106	.346	40
Milwaukee Brewers	96	66	.593	--
Pittsburgh Pirates	72	90	.444	24
St. Louis Cardinals	90	72	.556	6

Source: Major League Baseball, MLB.com

TABLE 5.7
Sort Data on the Most Meaningful Variable

A. Youth Television Watching		B. Youth Television Watching	
Percent of 9-year-olds who watch more than 5 hours of television per weekday		Percent of 9-year-olds who watch more than 5 hours of television per weekday	
Canada	14.9	**UNITED STATES**	**21.5**
Denmark	6.0	Spain	17.5
Finland	6.1	Canada	14.9
France	5.5	Netherlands	12.6
Germany	4.4	Ireland	11.8
Ireland	11.8	Italy	9.2
Italy	9.2	Finland	6.1
Netherlands	12.6	Denmark	6.0
Spain	17.5	France	5.5
Sweden	4.7	Sweden	4.7
UNITED STATES	**21.5**	Germany	4.4

Source: Uri Bronfenburger, et. al. *The State of Americans* (New York: The Free Press, 1996); qtd. In William Bennett, *The Index of Leading Cultural Indicators* (New York: Broadway Books, 1999), 230.

And in the league standings, the column in the standings labeled "Pct," for percent, is incorrect. "Percent" stands for "per 100." For the Cubs, ".438 percent" is the probability of the team ever winning a World Series (4 times every 1,000 years). Nevertheless, baseball is to be commended for not including an unnecessary leading zero (0.438) and using the percentage of games won (rather than "Games behind") for determining which team is in first place.

In table 5.2, the Illinois State Police should remove the decimal places from the "% Chg" row (reporting 11 percent rather than −10.9 percent) and there is no reason to include a decimal point to display the crime rate as 3,376.1.

Researchers who go beyond just plain data analysis and use correlation and regression analyses commonly display numbers with too many decimal places—presumably to add an aura of scientific precision. They also report far too many statistics in their tables. Again, the purpose seems to be to impress rather than explain, and the effect is to obscure the most important data in the tables. There is no need for any correlation coefficient, R-Square, standardized regression coefficient, or even a measure of statistical significance to be displayed with more than two decimal places.

Time

The professional education journal *Phi Delta Kappan* sponsors an annual poll of public attitudes about the nation's public schools.[6] Every year in numerous tables, their polling report displays data with the years going backward, with the most recent year's data in the first column on the left, as shown in table 5.8. Notice how difficult it is to discern whether the trend is increasing or decreasing.

In addition, for most polling data it is usually only necessary to report the percentages for one of the several possible answers to the question. The tables in Phi Delta Kappa's report are, in some respects, "look up" tables and

TABLE 5.8
Going Backwards in Time

"Do you favor or oppose allowing students and parents to choose to attend a private school at public expense?

	'02	'01	'99	'98	'97	'96	'95
Favor	46	34	39	41	44	44	36
Oppose	52	62	56	55	50	52	61
Don't know	2	4	5	4	6	4	3

Source: Rose and Gallup, *The 34th Annual Phi Delta Kappa/Gallup Poll*

including all three rows of data is appropriate, but most analyses of the data in research reports would only require data on either the percentage who favor or the percentage who oppose private school vouchers.

When each vertical column represents a different time period (such as in table 5.1), always display years in adjacent left to right columns. The same principle applies in the case of other ordered categories such as age groups, years of education, temperature ranges, height, or weight: the categories representing the highest values should generally appear on the right side of the table. Where time series trends are represented in a vertical column, place the most recent year at the bottom, unlike the way the Illinois State Police did it in table 5.2 with the 2009 data on top of the 2008.

When writing about numbers, as opposed to displaying them in a table, numbers can be rounded off even more. It is better to say that 50 million Americans are uninsured than 49.9. For table 5.5: The average black family income is $29,000, almost $20,000 less than that of white families.

Consistency

When a paper or report contains more than one table, the formatting should be consistent across tables: same fonts, same heading style, and same borders. If the four racial and ethnic categories are displayed as they are in table 5.5, they should be sorted in the same order, despite the sorting rule, in similar tables using the same categories (see the race categories in chapter 2).

Combining Tables

While cramming too much data and too many different kinds of data into a single table should be avoided, one should look for opportunities to combine several tables into one.

Table 5.9, derived from Christina Hoff Sommers' book *The War against Boys,* nicely summarizes a lot of data in a single table. A typical master's thesis containing the same data would display the data in six tables and add a lot of statistical measures that would not add to the data interpretation at all. The basic format used here is ideal for presenting cross-tabular survey data when a single variable is cross-tabulated against several others.

Sommers uses these data to make two points. The first is that teachers favor girls over boys. The second, more subtle point is conveyed in the title: that the American Association of University Women, who conducted the original survey (and who sponsored a report arguing that girls are ignored by teachers), suppressed the release of these data.[7] A less argumentative title

TABLE 5.9

Unpublished AAUW Data from the 1990 Self- Esteem Survey

	Responses by sex (%)	
	Girls' perception	Boys' perception
Who do teachers think are smarter?		
Boys	13	26
Girls	81	69
Other response	5	5
Who do teachers punish more often?		
Boys	92	90
Girls	5	8
Other response	3	2
Who do teachers compliment more		
Boys	7	15
Girls	89	81
Other response	5	4
Who do teachers like to be around?		
Boys	12	21
Girls	80	73
Other response	8	6
Who do teachers pay more attention		
Boys	33	29
Girls	57	64
Other response	10	7
Who do teachers call on more often?		
Boys	35	36
Girls	57	59
Other response	8	5

Source: Christina Hoff Sommers. *The War Against Boys: How Misguided Feminism is Harming Our Young Men* (Simon and Schuster, 2000), p. 42. original source of data: American Association of University Women. Greenberg-Lake Full Data Report: Expectation and Aspirations: Gender roles and Gender Self Esteem (Washington, D.C.: AAUW, 1990), p. 18.

for the table might have been "Boys' and Girls' Perceptions of Teachers' Gender Partiality."

Highlighting Comparisons

The purpose of properly sorting the data, correctly arranging the rows and columns, combining what could be multiple tables into one, and other efficiency rules is to allow the reader to quickly grasp the most meaningful comparisons that the data allow. Highlighting critical numbers in a table can serve the same purpose. On the assumption that the data are being presented to a U.S. audience, the United States is shown in a large bold font in table 5.10, which, by the way, reveals a familiar pattern: The United States is spending the most but not getting much for it.

Lines

A common and simple table format is used in most of the tables on these pages. It includes thin lines under the title and column headings and under the main body of data. Often, the title is in bold. Putting the headings in bold is advised only if they are very short headings, and not if it is inconsistent with the format of other tables in the report. The tables include only horizontal lines. This is due partly to the Modern Language Association (MLA) style guidelines, which were originally designed for manuscripts prepared with manual typewriters, but vertical lines are usually unnecessary.

MLA and the American Psychological Association (APA) style guidelines recommend that table titles be italicized (one of the few recent acknowledgments that manual typewriters are no longer in use). Both the title and the table number, which appears above the title, are aligned to the left. These style recommendations, however, are for papers that are not in final form—that is, manuscripts that will later be formatted by a publisher. The MLA style guide also specifies that tables (and the manuscript text) be double-spaced and that the tables and charts be placed at the end of the manuscript; this is for the convenience of manuscript typesetters and not for readers. (I am perplexed as to how it might be helpful in any case.)

TABLES, TEXT, AND AUDIENCES

The general purpose of a table is to present numerical information more efficiently than it can be expressed in the text. There are no hard-and-fast rules stating when a table is appropriate, but a paragraph with more than four or five numbers usually cries out for a table.

Similarly, charts should be used when they can more efficiently convey the ideas about numerical information than a table. Tables are usually preferred to charts when a very precise representation of the numbers is needed. Daily stock quotes and sports statistics are thus rarely presented in

Table 5.10
Higher Education: Spending and Degree Completion, OECD Nations

Tertiary Spending % of GDP, 2008	% of age group with College degrees (2009)		Graduation rates* (2009)
	25-34	56-64	
United States 2.7	Korea 63	Israel 45	Slovak Republic 61
Korea 2.6	Canada 56	United States 41	Iceland 51
Canada 2.5	Japan 56	Canada 41	Poland 50
Chile 2.2	Ireland 48	New Zealand 34	New Zealand 50
Finland 1.7	Norway 47	Estonia 33	Australia 49
Denmark 1.7	New Zealand 47	Australia 29	United Kingdom 48
Norway 1.7	United Kingdom 45	Finland 29	Denmark 47
Israel 1.6	Australia 45	United Kingdom 29	Ireland 47
New Zealand 1.6	Denmark 45	Switzerland 28	Finland 44
Sweden 1.6	France 43	Netherlands 27	Netherlands 42
Netherlands 1.5	Israel 43	Japan 27	Norway 41
Australia 1.5	Belgium 42	Norway 27	Japan 40
Poland 1.5	Sweden 42	Sweden 27	Portugal 40
Japan 1.5	United States 41	Denmark 26	Czech Republic 38
Ireland 1.4	Netherlands 40	Germany 25	United States 38
France 1.4	Switzerland 40	Belgium 23	Israel 37
Belgium 1.4	Finland 39	Iceland 23	Canada 37
Portugal 1.3	Spain 38	Ireland 20	Sweden 36
Austria 1.3	Estonia 37	France 18	Italy 33
Estonia 1.3	Iceland 36	Slovenia 17	Switzerland 31
Switzerland 1.3	Poland 35	Chile 17	Hungary 30
Iceland 1.3	Chile 35	Spain 17	Austria 29
Mexico 1.2	Slovenia 30	Hungary 16	Germany 28
Spain 1.2	Germany 26	Austria 16	Spain 27
United Kingdom 1.2	Hungary 25	Korea 13	Slovenia 27
Czech Republic 1.2	Portugal 23	Poland 13	Turkey 21
Germany 1.2	Austria 21	Slovak Republic 12	Mexico 19
Slovenia 1.1	Slovak Republic 21	Czech Republic 11	
Italy 1.0	Czech Republic 20	Italy 10	
Slovak Republic .9	Mexico 20	Mexico 10	
Hungary .9	Italy 20	Portugal 7	

*Degrees awarded/ % of population at typical graduation age
Source: OECD, *Education at a Glance, 2011*

bar charts. Time series trend data of more than five time points is generally better displayed in a time series chart than in a table.

One should strive to balance and integrate the tabular presentations with the textual discussion of the numerical evidence. Beware of "orphan tables": tables that are not referenced in the text. Although academic audiences (e.g., your professors) are sometimes impressed by richly detailed tabular presentations (and by dense and impenetrable writing), too many tables and too many numbers may turn off lay readers. In writing directed at general audiences, tables should contain the minimum data necessary to support the conclusions presented in the text. More sophisticated audiences, who might draw their own additional conclusions from a table, will appreciate more detail. When writing about data that are accompanied by tables and graphs, do not make "The table . . ." or "The figure . . ." the subject of your sentences: "Table 5.9 summarizes students' perceptions of teacher bias." Better to get right to the point: "Both boys and girls clearly perceive that teachers favor girls over boys (table 5.9)." This rule is regularly violated in this and the next chapter only because tables are in fact the subject of this chapter, and thus the sentences.

NOTES

1. Quoted in Howard Wainer, *Graphic Discovery* (Princeton, NJ: Princeton University Press, 2005), 9.

2. Illinois State Police, *Crime in Illinois* (reports from 1997 through 2009), September 27, 2011, at http://www.isp.state.il.us/crime/ucrhome.cfm.

3. Gary King, "Replication, Replication," *PS: Political Science and Politics* 28 (September 1995): 443–99.

4. Howard Wainer, "Improving Tabular Display: With NAEP Tables as Examples and Inspirations," *Journal of Educational and Behavioral Statistics* 22 (1997): 1–30.

5. Wainer, "Improving Tabular Display."

6. Lowell C. Rose and Alec M. Gallup, *The 34th Annual Phi Delta Kappa/Gallup Poll of the Public's Attitudes toward the Public Schools,* 2002, at http://www.pdkintl.org/kappan/k0209pol.htm.

7. Christina Hoff Sommers, *The War against Boys: How Misguided Feminism Is Harming Our Young Men* (New York: Simon & Schuster, 2000), 42.

CHAPTER 6

The Graphical Display of Data

Good information design is clear thinking made visible, while bad design is stupidity in action.

—EDWARD TUFTE, *VISUAL EXPLANATIONS*

A CHART PROVIDES a graphical display of numerical information that otherwise would be presented in a table. Ideally, a chart should convey ideas about the data that would not be readily apparent if they were displayed in a table or as text. Designing good charts, however, presents more challenges than tabular display, as it draws on the talents of both the scientist and the artist. You have to know and understand your data, but you also need a good sense of how the reader will visualize the chart's graphical elements.

GENERAL PRINCIPLES OF GRAPHIC DISPLAY

The two standards for tabular design—the *efficient* display of meaningful and *unambiguous* data—apply to charts as well. As with tables, it is crucial to good charting to choose meaningful data, to define precisely what the numbers represent, and to present the data in a manner that allows the reader to quickly grasp what the data mean. Data ambiguity in charts and tables results from the failure to define precisely just what the numbers in the presentation represent. Every dot on a scatterplot, every point on a time series line, every bar on a bar chart represents a number (actually, in the case of a scatterplot, two numbers). It is the job of the chart's text to tell the reader what each of those numbers means.

Two problems arise in charting that are less common in tabular displays. Poor or deliberately deceptive choices in graphic design can provide a distorted picture of the numbers and relationships they represent. A more common problem is that charts are often designed in ways that hide what the data might tell us or distract the reader from quickly discerning the meaning of the numerical evidence presented in the chart. Two classic texts on the graphical display of numbers, Darrell Huff's *How to Lie with Statistics*[1] and Edward Tufte's *The Visual Display of Quantitative Information*,[2] define the standards for effective data presentation and describe what can go wrong when basic principles are violated.

Huff's little paperback, first published in 1954 and reissued many times thereafter, contained many illustrations of graphical distortions of data. One graphic represented the growth in the number of milk cows in the United States (figure 6.1). The height of the cows represents the growth from 8 million cows in 1860 to 25 million in 1936. The 1936 cow is thus three times the height of the 1860 cow, but the 1936 cow is also three times as wide, taking up nine times the area of the page. Moreover, the graphic is a depiction of a three-dimensional figure; when we take the depth of the cow into account, she is twenty-seven times larger in volume in 1936. Later, Tufte developed the "lie factor" statistic, a numerical measure of the data distortion. Here, representing a number that is three times larger in magnitude with an image that is twenty-seven times larger produces a lie factor of nine.

Such visual distortions are not as common as they once were, but modern computer technology has made possible all sorts of new ways of lying with charts. Consider, for example, a *Wall Street Journal* editorial titled "No Politician Left Behind,"[3] containing two charts, similar to those reconstructed in figure 6.2a. The data display makes the case that American students' academic achievement has not improved, despite a doubling of education spending over a fourteen-year period.

Figure 6.1. U.S. Milk Cows.

25 million___

8 million___

1860   1936

Source: adapted from Huff and Giles.

Figure 6.2a. Money for Nothing: Education Spending Rises but Test Scores Are Flat.

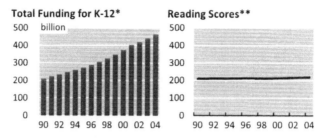

* Federal, state, and local spending, excludes special education.
**4th-grade NAEP reading scores: scores above 200 imply an ability to understand, combine ideas and make inferences based on short, uncomplicated passages about specific or sequentially related information.
Sources: National Center for Education Statistics, NAEP Data Explorer.

Part of the deception here is cherry-picking. Note that the spending is not adjusted for inflation and/or for the increase in the number of students. More deceptively, the right-hand chart uses a 500-point scale to depict the fourth-grade reading scores on the National Assessment of Educational Progress tests that are given to fourth-grade, eighth-grade, and junior-year high school students every two or three years. When the NAEP calculates the grades on the tests, all those students are measured on the same scale. No fourth grader could ever score 500 on the test. If the fourth-grade scores had risen to just 300, their reading level would be significantly higher than the average high school junior.

Reconstructing the *Journal*'s charts with the spending data adjusted for inflation and the number of students and the reading score chart re-scaled suggests a much different conclusion (figure 6.2b). Spending has increased 24 percent in real terms, still a significant increase but not the 100 percent that the *Journal*'s chart depicted. On a 20-point scale we see a steady increase in the average test score.

Figure 6.2b. Money Matters: Education Spending Rises and So Do Test Scores.

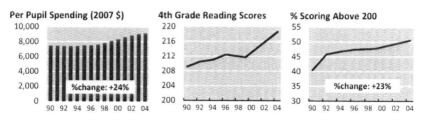

It would not be appropriate to calculate a percentage change in the average score because the scale does not have an absolute zero base (this, similar to a Fahrenheit temperature scale), but when we calculate the percentage change in students scoring above the 200-level standard, the increase in reading proficiency is almost equal to the increased investment in education.[4]

In truth, such distortions are rare in the *Journal*, and many features in the graphic design of the two charts in figure 6.2a (which is a close approximation of the original) are commendable. The side-by-side charts are a clearly understandable way of presenting two time series trends that are measured on different scales. The charts are small and contain only the text necessary to describe the data (and maybe to make their editorial point). The light gray background and white gridlines do not overpower the depiction of the data. The choice of a bar chart for the spending data and the line chart for the reading scores was made with good reason, consistent with the *Journal*'s graphical standards.[5] The data could have been presented in a table (much of the *Journal* consists of tabular presentation of stock market data), but it would not have conveyed the basic point to the reader as quickly.

One of Edward Tufte's many contributions to the art and science of graphic design was to stress the virtue of efficient data presentation. Tufte would second Emperor Joseph II's famous complaint to a young composer: "Too many notes, Mozart." His fundamental rule of efficient graphical design is to "minimize the ink-to-data ratio" by eliminating any elements from the chart that do not aid in conveying what the numbers mean. Tufte's advice to those who would chart data is essentially the same advice offered by William Strunk and E. B. White to would-be writers:

> A sentence should contain no unnecessary words, a paragraph no unnecessary sentences for the same reason that a drawing should have no unnecessary lines and a machine no unnecessary parts.[6]

Just as the purpose of any statistic is to simplify, to represent in one number a larger set of numbers, the purpose of a chart is to simplify numerical comparisons: to represent several numerical comparisons in a single graphic. The most common errors in chart design are to include elements in the graphical display that have nothing to do with presenting the numerical comparisons.

THE COMPONENTS OF A CHART

Most charts have three basic components: the text, the axes, and the graphical elements. The textual labels—the chart's title, axis titles, axis labels,

Rules for Charting Data

- A chart should be self-explanatory. The reader should not be required to read a written summary of the data to figure out what the chart means.
- Define data precisely and concisely. The text in the chart ought to precisely define what each number represented by the graphical elements of the chart means. Avoid redundant and unnecessary text.
- Present meaningful numerical comparisons that convey interesting ideas. Ideas are conclusions drawn from numerical comparisons; the more comparisons that can be effectively presented the better.
- Present the numerical information efficiently. Avoid elements in the charts' text and graphics that are not necessary to represent and explain the data. Minimize the use of graphical elements that are not necessary to depict the data. Always avoid 3-D effects.
- Organize the data. Sort data on the most meaningful variable and never sort data alphabetically.
- Show the data. Do not let the design, scale, and graphical elements of the chart hide the numerical information.
- Be honest. Avoid graphical distortions.
- Choose the appropriate type of chart for the data. Don't let the most convenient button on the spreadsheet determine your choice of a chart.
- Be consistent. Across many charts, use similar fonts, graphical elements, and formatting (this rule is violated in this chapter in order to illustrate many alternatives).

legends, and notes—define the numbers. The chart's graphical elements—the bars, pie slices, and lines, and their size and position on the graphic—represent the magnitudes of the numbers. The y axis (and sometimes the x axis) defines the scale of the numbers represented in the chart (figure 6.3).

Chart Titles

In academic writing, the chart title should define the data series without imposing a data interpretation on the reader. In journalistic writing, such as is the case with the *Wall Street Journal*'s chart "Money for Nothing," above, a chart title will sometimes state the conclusion the writer would have the reader draw from the chart. Often, the units of measurement are specified

Figure 6.3. The Components of a Chart.

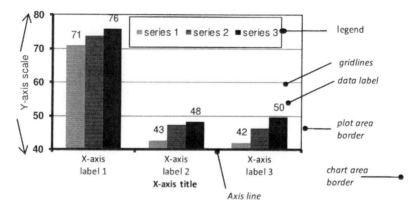

at the end of the title after a colon, or in parentheses in a subtitle (e.g., "constant dollars," "% of GDP," or "billions of U.S. dollars"). Unless the years or dates are displayed on the *x* axis, the title should include some indication of the date of the data.

Axis Titles and Labels

Axis titles should be succinct and not used at all if they merely repeat what is clear from the main title or axis labels. If a chart title indicates that the data are measured as a "% of GDP," it is not necessary to repeat the wording in the *y* axis title that is already in the chart title. Using "Year" as the *x* axis title in time series charts is redundant when the *x* axis labels (e.g., "1990, 1991, 1992") clearly represent years. Many charts (the vast majority of scatterplots) label the *y* axis with vertical text. This has the advantage of minimizing white space and allowing more space for the depiction of the data, but it has the disadvantage of being harder to read. A nice alternative is the ingenious placement of the word "billion" in figure 6.2a. It is also common to see *x* axis labels at a 45° or 90° angle. This should be avoided.

Axis Scale

The value or magnitude of the main graphical elements of a chart is defined by the labeling of the *y* axis scale and data increments that define the gridlines. A common mistake is to include too many increments in the scale: Using more than five is usually not a good idea. Where possible, the increments should be spaced in whole numbers and rounded off to thousands or billions as appropriate.

Data Labels

Data labels serve the same function as the increments on the axis scale and do so by more precisely identifying individual data points. Note that if all the points in the graphic are represented by data labels, the y axis labels—and the gridlines—are unnecessary (see figure 3.1).

Legends

Legends are used when a chart has more than one data series; they are usually only needed for bar charts. With time series charts, labeling the actual trendline usually works better than a separate legend and sometimes eliminates the need to distinguish the lines with additional markers (figure 6.9, below). If legends are used, they should correspond to the ordering of the graphical elements they represent.

Gridlines

If used at all, gridlines should use as little ink as possible so as not to overwhelm the main graphical elements of the chart.

Sources

Specifying the source of the data is important for proper academic citation, but it can also give knowledgeable readers who are familiar with common data sources important insights into the reliability and validity of the data. For example, knowing that crime statistics come from the FBI rather than the National Criminal Victimization Survey can be a crucial bit of information.

Throughout this book, I have used short titles for the sources, usually just an agency name or the agency name and title of an agency's major publication. This is common practice in newspaper and magazine stories, but it can be very frustrating for readers who find they have a need to track down the original data from a source as generic as "Census Bureau." In term papers, theses, and academic writing, far more complete citations are necessary. But even a full citation in a printed source is less than ideal: You can't click on a printed link and browse the data source. Almost all of the data depicted in this book were obtained on the Internet, and an active link to the original data is the best way for researchers to check sources or to find similar data. For this, see the companion website to the book: http://pol.illinoisstate.edu/jpda.

Other Chart Elements

The amount of ink used to depict nondata elements of a chart that are not necessary for defining the meaning and values of the data should be kept to a minimum. Chart area borders, plot area borders, and chart-and-plot area shading are unnecessary. Keep the shading of the graphical elements simple, and avoid the visually distracting diagonal hatching of bars and pie slices. In many of the charts that follow, even the vertical line defining the y axis has been removed, following the commendable charting standards of the *Economist* magazine.

Three-dimensional bar charts and pie charts are an unforgivable violation of Tufte's "minimize the ink-to-data ratio" rule. They are visually distracting, offer a less precise representation of the numbers, make meaningful comparisons of the numbers more difficult, and often produce graphical distortions of the data. The most serious violation of the rule, however, is "ChartJunk," distracting pictures or images that are meant to decorate the graphics.

Printed charts should have a primarily white or light gray background, but for charts used in slideshows, it is sometimes best to use a dark (usually blue) background and bright primary colors (white, yellow, red, and light blue) for the text and chart elements.

TYPES OF CHARTS

Most charts are a variation on one of four basic types: pie charts, bar charts, time series charts, and scatterplots. Choosing the right type of chart depends on the characteristics of the data and the relationships you want to display.

Pie Charts

Pie charts represent the distribution of the categorical components of a single variable (or data series) and should only be used for data that add up to a meaningful 100 percent total. It would not be correct to use a pie chart for black-white-Hispanic categories if Hispanics were included in the

---

Rules for Pie Charts

- Avoid using pie charts.
- Use pie charts only for data that add up to some meaningful 100% total.
- Never ever use three-dimensional pie charts; they are even worse than two-dimensional ones.
- Avoid using legends to label the pie slices.
- Avoid forcing comparisons across more than one pie chart.
- Use pie charts only if you are really interested in showing the size of one slice or multiple slices that add up to a meaningful fraction of the total.
- If given a choice between a doughnut, cylinder, cone, radar, pyramid, or pie chart, by all means use the pie chart.

---

black-white racial categories. Even the composition data depicted by a pie chart are often not what a writer should be using. It is usually more meaningful to indicate what percentage of whites, blacks, and Hispanics are poor or uninsured than to indicate the percentage of the poor or of the uninsured that are white, black, and Hispanic. Even then, there are usually better ways to depict data than with a pie chart.

Pie charts contain more ink than is necessary to display the data, and the slices provide a poor representation of the magnitude of the data points. Do you remember as a kid trying to decide which slice of your birthday cake was the largest? It is more difficult for the eye to discern the relative size of pie slices than it is to assess relative bar length.

For some reason, pie charts are a favorite way of displaying budget outlays and receipts. A popular American public policy textbook[7] uses a chart similar to figure 6.4a to represent federal expenditures by function. The supposed advantage of a pie graphic is that the design is simple—but look carefully at the pie and try to figure out which category has the biggest slice.

Note that all the numerical information in the graphic is actually contained in the legend. If the information had been sorted in any meaningful order, one could readily figure out what was going on with the data without looking at the pie. A far simpler solution that uses less ink but conveys more information is the properly sorted bar chart (figure 6.4b).

At best, pie charts can be used to make a very simple point when the focus is on just one or a combination of two slices, as in figure 6.5a where we see that most of the uninsured, and an increasing proportion of the

Figure 6.4a. Federal Spending by Category, 2010 (percent).

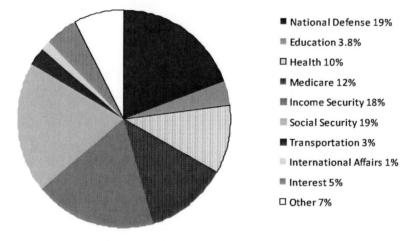

- National Defense 19%
- Education 3.8%
- Health 10%
- Medicare 12%
- Income Security 18%
- Social Security 19%
- Transportation 3%
- International Affairs 1%
- Interest 5%
- Other 7%

Source: Office of Management and Budget, Budget of the U.S. Government, fiscal year 2011.

Figure 6.4b. Federal Expenditures by Function, 2010 (billions).

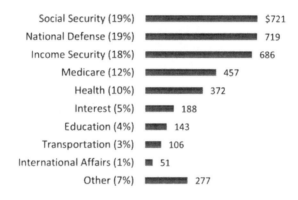

Social Security (19%) — $721
National Defense (19%) — 719
Income Security (18%) — 686
Medicare (12%) — 457
Health (10%) — 372
Interest (5%) — 188
Education (4%) — 143
Transportation (3%) — 106
International Affairs (1%) — 51
Other (7%) — 277

uninsured, work full-time. Still, it takes a lot of ink to display just three data points in each pie. It is usually a bad idea to force the reader to draw comparisons across two pie charts; using two pies to represent the budget categories in figure 6.4a at two points in time would be hopeless.

Be precise when writing about pie chart data. Many readers, even very educated readers, misinterpret pie charts and would wrongly conclude from the pies in figure 6.5a that people who work full-time are more likely to be uninsured than those who do not work.

For placement of the slices, think of the pie as a clock with the key slice starting at 12 o'clock. The three slices in figure 6.5a are placed in sequential

Figure 6.5a. Employment Status of the Uninsured, Age 16–64: 1999, 2009.

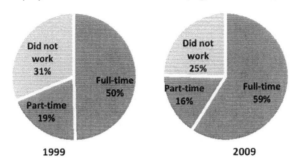

1999   2009

Source: Census Bureau, Current Population Survey: 1999, 2009.

order for a reason. If you really have to use a pie chart—not that you ever really have to—labeling the slices is much better than using a legend.

Cut the fat! Doughnuts are just as fattening as pies. A doughnut chart depicting two years of federal spending would be hopeless. The redeeming attribute of the doughnut graphic is that it displays more than one data series in a single chart. If, and only if, the series have a few categories of approximately the same size, identifying the numerical comparison is not too difficult if the magnitude of the slices can be read like a clock face. Because the area of the inner doughnut is much smaller than the outer, there is some graphical distortion.

Despite all my warnings, people like pie charts. Readers expect to see one or two pie charts similar to those in figure 6.4a at the very beginning of an annual agency budget report, but it would be a mistake to rely on several pie charts for the primary data analysis in any report.

Figure 6.5b. Doughnuts.

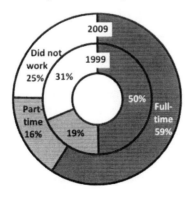

For those who would ignore all the advice given here and insist that good charts must look pretty, the most recent version of the Microsoft Excel® charting software (in Office 2011) will satisfy all your foolish desires. It features 3-D pie charts that gleam and glisten like Christmas tree ornaments or explode like Fourth of July fireworks, to say nothing about what you can do with the 3-D pie chart's pretty, but also pretty useless, cousins: the doughnut, cylinder, cone, radar, and pyramid charts.

One interesting variation on pie charting does offer an excellent visual representation of certain kinds of data and is similar in some respects to the *Consumer Reports* product evaluation charts. Table 6.1 is a revised version of a chart that appeared in the *Economist* in the 1980s, when countries across the world were beginning to privatize government-owned sectors of the economy.[8] When the data are sorted (the original *Economist* presentation was sorted alphabetically!) so that the countries with the most publicly held industries are at the top and the industries most commonly publicly held at the left, the tabulation forms a Guttman scale, allowing one to quickly discern the relative extent of public ownership across countries and industries.

Bar Charts

Bar charts typically display the relationship between one or more categorical variables with one or more quantitative variables represented by the length of the bars. The categorical variables are usually defined by the categories displayed on the X axis and, if there is more than one data series, by the legend.

Bar charts are not a very efficient method of data presentation; they often contain little data, a lot of ink, and rarely reveal ideas that cannot be presented much more simply in a table. Minimizing the ink-to-data ratio

---

Rules for Bar Charts

- Minimize the ink; do not use 3-D effects.
- Sort the data on the most significant variable.
- Time should always go left to right.
- Use rotated bar charts (but never for time series) if there are more than eight to ten categories or to avoid using vertical text.
- Minimize the use of colors and shadings.
- Place legends inside or below the plot area.
- Beware of scaling distortions.

TABLE 6.1
Government Ownership of Key Economic Sectors, 1985

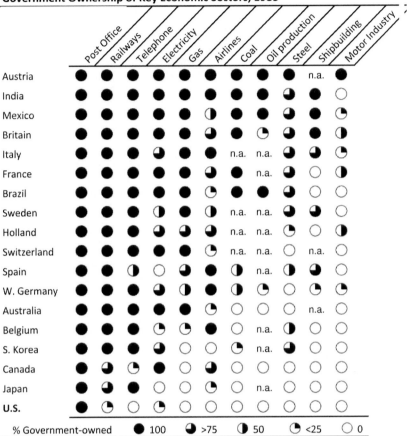

	Post Office	Railways	Telephone	Electricity	Gas	Airlines	Coal	Oil production	Steel	Shipbuilding	Motor Industry
Austria	●	●	●	●	●	●	●	●	●	n.a.	●
India	●	●	●	●	●	●	●	●	◕	●	○
Mexico	●	●	●	●	●	◑	●	●	◕	●	◔
Britain	●	●	●	●	●	◔	●	◔	◕	●	◑
Italy	●	●	●	◔	●	●	n.a.	n.a.	◕	◕	◔
France	●	●	●	●	●	◔	●	n.a.	◕	○	◑
Brazil	●	●	●	●	●	◔	●	●	◕	○	○
Sweden	●	●	●	◑	●	◑	n.a.	n.a.	◕	◕	○
Holland	●	●	●	◕	◕	◕	n.a.	n.a.	◔	○	◑
Switzerland	●	●	●	●	●	◔	n.a.	n.a.	○	n.a.	○
Spain	●	●	◑	○	◕	●	◑	n.a.	◑	◕	○
W. Germany	●	●	●	◕	◑	●	◑	◔	○	◔	◔
Australia	●	●	●	●	●	◔	○	○	○	n.a.	○
Belgium	●	●	●	◔	◔	●	○	n.a.	◑	○	○
S. Korea	●	●	●	◕	○	○	◔	n.a.	◕	○	○
Canada	●	◕	◔	●	○	◕	○	○	○	○	○
Japan	●	◕	●	○	○	◔	○	n.a.	○	○	○
U.S.	●	◔	○	◔	○	○	○	○	○	○	○

% Government-owned ● 100 ◕ >75 ◑ 50 ◔ <25 ○ 0

Source: *The Economist*, 12/21/85

is especially important in the case of bar charts. Never use a 3-D bar chart. Keep the gridlines faint. Display no more than seven numbers on the *y* axis scale. If there are fewer than five bars, consider using data labels rather than a *y* axis scale; it doesn't make sense to use a five-numbered *y* axis scale when the exact values can be shown with four numbers.

As with tables, sorting the data on the most significant variable greatly eases the interpretation of the data. In 2002, the annual report of the Illinois Board of Higher Education[9] (conflict of interest disclosure: my employer) contained a graphic depiction of tuition and fees at the twelve public universities over which it rules (figure 6.6a). The 3-D effect is mostly just annoying and the white border for the undergraduate bars was an unfortunate choice; but the most egregious shortcoming with the chart is the alphabetical sorting.

Properly sorted (figure 6.6b), one can quickly see which universities charge the highest, lowest, and above and below median tuition. And there's more. Note how the universities in the middle (especially including my direct employer, ISU) charge undergraduates more than graduate students. This should be surprising, since it costs far more to educate graduate students than undergraduate students, who are generally taught in much larger classes and by lower-paid instructors. The reason for the disparity, I suspect, is that the middle-range schools, and the faculty who teach in those schools, aspire to be graduate research universities like the two University of Illinois campuses (UIUC and UIC) and are willing to have the undergraduates subsidize that goal.

The same IBHE report also contains a graphic depicting higher education enrollment trends (figure 6.7a). Right away you notice the 3-D effect,

Figure 6.6a. Tuition and Fees, Illinois Public Universities, 2001.

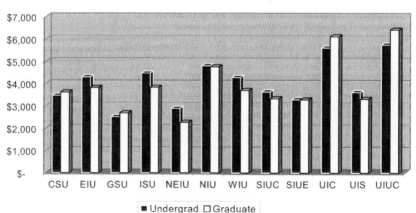

Source: IBHE, Annual Report, 2002.

Figure 6.6b. Tuition and Fees, Illinois Public Universities, 2001.

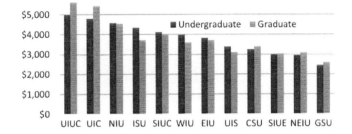

and it takes some time to figure out if the taller bars rise above the 700,000 mark. But look carefully at the *x* axis and notice the year 2000 on the far left.

The graphic effectively makes the point that community college enrollments are at least twice as high as either public or private enrollments, but it is particularly poor at depicting the trends in enrollments over time. Notice also how flat the trends are. Even if time were going the right way, it is not easy to tell which trend is increasing or decreasing. Potentially misleading scaling effects occur when a bar chart (or a line chart, as we will see) has two data series with numbers of a substantially different magnitude, minimizing the variation in the data series containing the smaller numbers.

Figure 6.7a. Total 12–Month Headcounts.

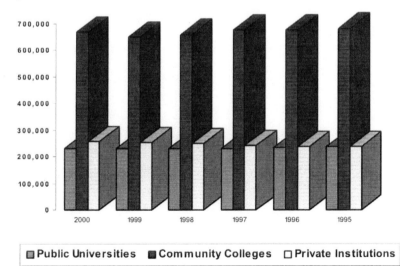

Source: IBHE, Annual Report, 2002.

By using comparable data (the only available data: fall semester headcounts rather than twelve-month headcounts), eliminating the 3-D effects, sorting time from left to right, removing the community college data series, and adjusting the bottom of the scale, we see something in figure 6.7b that the IBHE chart obscured. Private institution enrollments are increasing, while public university enrollments are flat. Here, there is reason to believe that the data deception, if not intentional, is at least self-serving. It is within the scope of the IBHE's responsibility to advocate that public universities increase their enrollments, but the board has been quiet. That these enrollment trends serve the interests of both the private colleges (which gain revenue from more enrollments) and public institutions (where state support does not keep pace with enrollments) more than they serve the public interest may have something to do with that.

There is some debate among charting enthusiasts as to whether charts should include zero as the base for the y axis. Critics of not using a zero-base insist that reducing the scale, as in figure 6.7b, exaggerates the variation in the data. Here, the private institutions' bar for 2000 is more than twice as high as the public university bar, but the private institution enrollments are only about 8 percent higher. The "lie factor" is 14. Jane E. Miller argues that y axis scales should start at zero with "rare exceptions" (none of her charts are an exception).[10] Howard Wainer, however, insists that any choice of scale is arbitrary. "Automatic rules," he says, "do not always work; wisdom and honesty are always required."[11] The downside of using the zero base is that it can hide significant variations in the data. I do not think that the depiction in figure 6.7b is at all unfair. It is fair to say, I think, that private institutions have accounted for most of the growth in university and college enrollments in the state, and the graph shows that well. Miller suggests that calculating annual change and using a zero base would be preferable, but as we see in figure 6.7c, this exaggerates the differences even more.

The *Wall Street Journal Guide to Information Graphics*[12] agrees with Miller on the zero base, but only for bar charts, and deems the use of a zero

Figure 6.7 (b, c). Fall Headcount Enrollment, Annual % Change, 1995–2000.

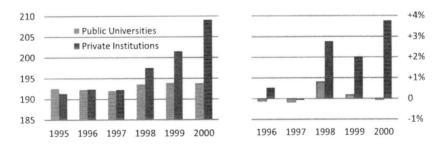

Figure 6.8. Illinois Public Schools, Racial and Ethnic Composition, 2006.

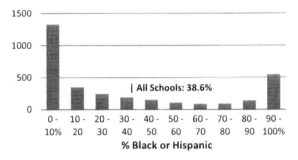

Source: Illinois State Board of Education, 2006 Report Card.

base unnecessary for time series line charts. The reasoning is that the area of the bars, not the height, conveys the magnitude of the represented numbers. As a general rule, the *Journal* uses bar charts for "counts," such as auto sales or total revenue and expenditures, while line charts are used to represent prices and rates (as in the "Money for Nothing" chart, figure 6.2a). Consistent with this, bar charts should only be used for data that have a meaningful zero base (referred to as a "ratio" level of measurement). Temperature (5 degrees is not five times warmer than 0 degrees), NAEP, SAT and ACT test scores, and most index measures based on combinations of several indicators (such as the Transparency Index, Human Rights Index, or the Index of Leading Economic Indicators) should not be depicted with bar or area charts.

Bar charts (and area charts) do have a visual advantage over line charts when the *y* axis spans positive and negative values, as is illustrated with the bar and line charts in figure 1.1.

Histograms are a form of bar chart used to display the distribution of a continuous variable along a set of defined categorical ranges. The histogram in figure 6.8 provides a graphic depiction of the segregation of black and Hispanic students in Illinois public schools. If there were very little segregation, most of the schools, the tallest bars, would have between 30 percent and 50 percent of student body black or Hispanic. Instead, more than half of the state's approximately 3,200 schools have a student body that is either more than 90 percent, or less than 10 percent, black or Hispanic.

Times Series Line Charts

The time series chart is one of the most efficient means of displaying large amounts of data in ways that provide for meaningful analysis.

Rules for Time Series (Line) Charts

- Always display time on the *x* axis from left to right.
- Display as much data with as little ink as possible.
- Make sure the reader can clearly distinguish the lines for separate data series.
- Directly label the lines rather than use legends.
- Beware of scaling effects.
- Use deflated data (e.g., inflation-adjusted or % of GDP) when displaying fiscal or monetary data over time.
- Do not use line charts for unordered categorical data.

Time series data are often used to highlight important societal and political trends. In their 1976 book, *The Changing American Voter*, Norman Nie, Sidney Verba, and John Petrocik cited the steady decline in new voters affiliating with either political party as evidence of the increasing sophistication of the electorate.[13]

One intriguing *Economist* chart feature, employed in some of the time series charts in this book (figures 1.2–1.5) is to place the *y* axis on the right-hand side of time series charts, allowing the reader to more readily identify the last, most important, values in the trend. An alternative to this is to include a data label for the last data point on each trend (figure 6.9).

Scaling Effects As we have seen in several earlier examples, inappropriate scaling can both hide significant variation in the data and distort the magnitude of critical relationships. Nevertheless, the choice of any scale is most often a matter of judgment. As a general rule, a trend line should take up about two-thirds of the *y* axis scale.

The Public Agenda website,[14] which provides a great deal of social indicator data on a wide range of public issues, carries the zero base principle to its logical extreme: If not having a 0 percent as the base number is graphical distortion, then so too is not having 100 percent as the upper limit for the scale for indicators measured in percentages. The result is shown in figure 6.10a and is among the most blatant violations of Tufte's "show the data" directive. Rescaled in figure 6.10b (and without the annoying 45° angle on the *x* axis labels), the chart reveals much of the variation in international affairs spending that was hidden.

When two variables with numbers of different magnitudes are graphed on the same chart, the variable with the larger scale will generally appear to

Figure 6.9. Party Identification of Age Cohorts at Entrance into the Electorate, 1920–1972.

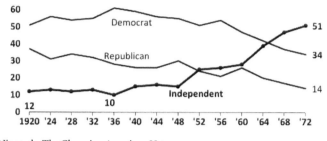

Source: Nie et al., *The Changing American Voter.*

have a greater degree of variation. The smaller-scale variable will appear relatively flat, even though the percentage change is the same. In figure 6.11a, ABCorp's stock seems to be growing much faster than that of XYZCom; yet the rate of increase is identical.

One solution to graphical scaling distortions is to use a logarithmic *y* axis scale. On a log scale, trend lines of different magnitudes that have the same percentage increase display the same increase in the height of the trend line, as shown with the same data graphed in figure 6.11b. In figure 1.5, a log scale was used for the infant mortality rate time series chart. Without the log scale, all the lines would merge into the bottom right-hand side of the graph.

Comparing federal outlays in figure 6.12 with and without the log scaling, we find that federal outlays in recent decades have actually increased at about the same percentage rate as they did in earlier decades. While the increased spending for World War II appears to be just a minor blip in the first chart, on a log scale it shows up as the most significant budget increase.

Figure 6.10 (a, b). International Affairs, % of Federal Outlays, 1970–2010.

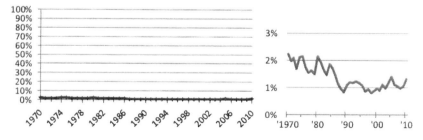

Source: Budget of the U.S. Government, 2012.

Figure 6.11 (a, b). Stock Prices of Two Companies.

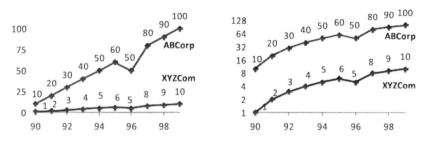

Nevertheless, unless one is writing for an audience of seismologists, log scales should be used cautiously. The statistically illiterate will not care what scale is used, but the statistically semiliterate are likely to take exception to log scales and to view them as an attempt at data distortion. In most cases, using some form of ratio measure is a better solution. In the case of the federal government outlays measure, a measure of outlays per capita, in constant dollars (e.g., adjusted for inflation), or outlays as a percentage of GDP would be preferable alternatives.

Stacked Bar and Area Charts

Stacked bar and area charts are sometimes useful, but with the wrong data or if incorrectly formatted they often work to hide meaningful information.

Figure 6.13a is a close approximation of a stacked area chart that appeared in the same public policy textbook that had the really bad pie chart.[15] It contains two errors unrelated to the use of the stacks. The title indicates that the data represent "thousands of wells drilled," which would suggest that the United States once drilled over 70 million wells. The axis, however, correctly labels "the number of wells drilled." To avoid the axis labeling limitations in the pre-2011 version of Microsoft Excel˙, whoever made the chart

Figure 6.12 (a, b). Federal Government Outlays, 1900–2010.

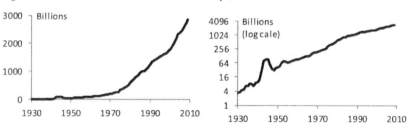

Source: Budget of the U.S. Government, 2012.

Rules for Stacked Charts

- Use stacked charts only if the data series are in a meaningful order.
- Each stack should represent a meaningful addition to the stacks below it.
- Sort the data so that the most meaningful data are on the bottom.

decided to use only the nine data points for which the axis labels are shown rather than include the annual data that their source provided after 1995.

The placement of the "dry holes" series at the bottom of the chart illustrates a common problem with stacking. One can readily discern how many wells were drilled and how many of them were dry holes, but it is difficult to figure out what is going on in terms of the number of gas and oil wells. The top of the middle stack represents the number of gas wells drilled plus the number of dry oil and gas wells drilled—not a meaningful addition.

The revised chart (figure 6.13b) includes all of the original data and reveals much that was hidden in the original chart. There is the precipitous drop in gas and oil exploration when energy prices fell during the 2009 recession (the Gulf oil spill came later, in April 2010). With dry holes on top of the stack and natural gas at the bottom, we can now see a couple of things that were hidden in the original representation. Natural gas wells (actually this is "successful natural gas wells") peaked at over 30 thousand in 2008, twice as many as had been drilled before 1998. The total number of successful oil and gas wells also peaked in 2008, reaching a level not seen since 1985. Still, the stacking has problems, particularly if the purpose of the chart were to support conclusions comparing oil with natural gas drilling.

Figure 6.13a. U.S. Domestic Oil and Gas Exploration, 1973–2009 (thousands of wells).

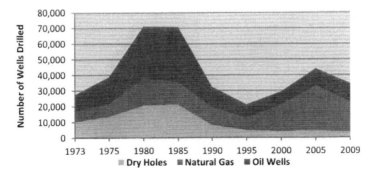

Source: U.S Energy Information Administration, Monthly Energy Review, April, 2010.

Figure 6.13b. U.S. Domestic Oil and Gas Exploration Wells Drilled, 1973–2009.

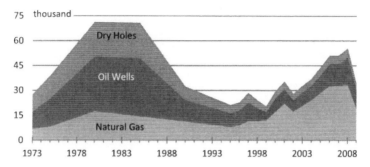

The Florida Department of Law Enforcement website[16] includes a stacked bar chart similar to the one in figure 6.14a, depicting the number of officers assaulted with and without injuries. With the injured officers at the top of the stacks, the height of each stack displays two data points: the number of officers assaulted without injury and the number of officers assaulted. The mistake here is to put the most important data on the top of the stack. In the revised chart (figure 6.14b), the two data points represented are the number of officers injured and the total number assaulted.

Scatterplots

The two-dimensional scatterplot is the most efficient medium for the graphical display of data. A simple scatterplot tells more about the relationship between two continuous (or interval-level) variables than any other method of presenting or summarizing such data.

Figure 6.14a. Officers Assaulted in Florida, 2000–2010.

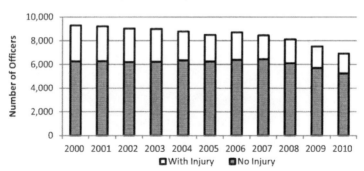

Source: Florida Department of Law Enforcement.

Figure 6.14b. Number of Officers Assaulted in Florida, 2000–2010.

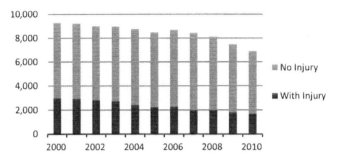

   With good labeling of the variables and cases and commonsense scaling of the *x* and *y* axes, not a lot can go wrong with a scatterplot, although extreme outliers on one or more of the variables can obscure patterns in the data.

   Figure 6.15 depicts the relationship between obesity (the independent variable) and life expectancy (the dependent variable). Note the conclusions that can be drawn from these data:

- There is a strong negative relationship between obesity and life expectancy.
- The United States scores the worst on both measures, Japan the best.
- Denmark is an "outlier" for some reason, having a much lower life expectancy than one would expect from its relatively low level of obesity. The opposite is true of Australia.

Rules for Scatterplots

- Use two interval-level variables.
- Fully define both variables with the axis titles.
- Use the chart title to identify both variables and the units of analysis (e.g., people, cities, or states).
- If there is an implied causal relationship between the variables, place the independent variable (the one that causes the other) on the *x* axis and the dependent variable (the one that may be caused by the other) on the *y* axis.
- Scale the axes to maximize the use of the plot area for displaying the data points.
- Use data labels rather than dots to identify the cases, if possible.

Figure 6.15. Obesity and Life Expectancy, 20 Wealthy OECD Nations.

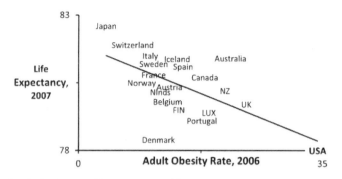

Sources: OECD, Society at a Glance, 2009; Health Data, 2010.

The trend line in figure 6.15, commonly referred to as the regression line, is the line that goes as close as possible to the points depicted on the scatterplot. For those who will go beyond the scope of this book, relationships such as this are often represented in a regression equation, in this case:

$$\text{Life expectancy} = 82 - (.11 \times \text{Obesity})$$

The equation means that, on average, each percentage increase in the obesity rate corresponds to a reduction in life expectancy of .11 years (or, 10 percent increase in obesity will reduce life expectancy by over one year).

Still another statistic, the correlation coefficient, or *r*, measures how close the countries are to the regression line on a scale of –1 to 0 to +1 (with 1 being a perfect positive relationship). Here the correlations coefficient is –.62, indicating a pretty strong negative relationship. If Australia and Denmark were excluded, the regression equation would have stayed about the same, but the correlation coefficient would have become –.81.

Going back to the two sabermetric scatterplots in chapter 1, the correlation of team batting average with total runs scored is +.81. The correlation between team on-base percentage and runs scored is a much stronger +.92.

Incorporating time series provides an interesting twist on the scatterplot. In figure 6.16a, we see South Africa enjoying both increasing economic prosperity and longer life expectancy from 1960 until 1981, when the economy collapsed under the pressure of worldwide economic sanctions against the apartheid regime. With the end of apartheid, the economy improved, but with the AIDS epidemic and the new regime's inept response to it, life expectancy fell. The data and the inspiration for figure 6.16a were obtained from the Gapminder World website,[17] which offers powerful interactive animations based on a large set of economic and social data for all the world's

Figure 6.16a. Life Expectancy and GDP Per Capita, South Africa, 1960–2008.

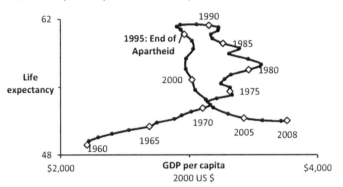

Source: Gapmider.org.

nations. The Google® Public Data Explorer website offers a very similar interactive display and a larger set of social indicator data.[18]

The time series scatterplot does not work well with some kinds of data. If the trends change rapidly from high to low values, the result can look like a plate of spaghetti. Whether plot is more readily interpretable than a standard two-variable line plot (figure 6.16b) probably depends on one's sense of artistic design. In this case, the image of the AIDS ribbon conveys a powerful message.

Boxplots

John W. Tukey invented the boxplot as a convenient method of displaying the distribution of interval-level variables.

The simple boxplot in figure 6.17 displays the four quartiles of the data, with the "box" comprising the two middle quartiles, separated by the

Figure 6.16b. Life Expectancy and GDP Per Capita (2000 US$), South Africa, 1960–2008.

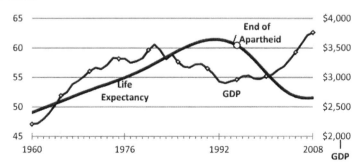

Rules for Boxplots

- A simple boxplot displays the median and four quartiles of data for an interval-level variable.
- Boxplots are best used for comparing the distribution of the same variable for two or more groups or two or more time points.
- Boxplots are an excellent means of displaying a single case compared to a large number of other cases.

median. Single lines extending above and below the box represent the upper and lower quartiles.

A single boxplot, as in figure 6.17, reveals much less about a data distribution than does a histogram. This is especially so in the case of distributions that are not concentrated around the median, as was the case with the school segregation data in figure 6.8.

The real advantage of the boxplot graphic comes through when several boxplots are used to compare the distribution of a variable across groups or over time.

Figure 6.17. Repeated Drunkenness: % of Boys, Ages 13–15, 24 OECD Nations, 2005.

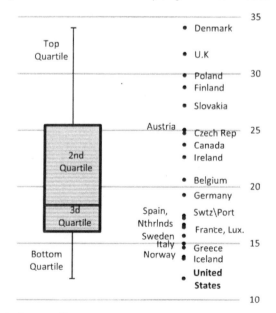

Source: OECD, Society at a Glance, 2009.

Figure 6.18. Infant Mortality Rates, U.S. and 33 OECD Nations (all OECD nations, excluding Turkey and Mexico), 1960–2008 (per 1,000 births) (log scale).

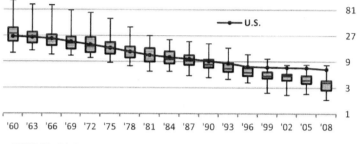

Source: OECD Health Data 2011.

An especially useful elaboration of the boxplot chart is to plot one or a few cases over a time series of boxplots to compare a single case to the overall distribution. Figure 6.18 depicts the same data as did figure 1.5, but with more countries (34 OECD nations, including the United States) and fewer time points (every three years).

The disadvantage of the boxplot is that it takes some explaining for audiences that are not familiar with the graphic, violating the principle that a graphic should be self-explanatory. Compare, for example, the textual discussion of figure 4.1 (the New York City murder rates and the large city boxplots) with the self-explanatory data depicted in the health care time series in figures 1.3, 1.4, and 1.5.

Sparklines

Edward Tufte's sparkline plots, which he describes as "intense, simple, word-sized graphics," illustrate his principles of graphic minimalism.[19] Each sparkline eliminates all the nondata graphical elements of the chart, providing a simple display of the variation in the trend and just enough numerical information to make meaningful comparisons. Used as a column in a table, the sparkline is a very efficient display of a large amount of information in a small space. In table 6.2, we can quickly discern that New York City has continued the downward trend in reported crimes since Mayor Giuliani left office. Despite this (or, maybe, this is because) arrests have increased.

Sparklines can also be used with area or bar charts (see table 9.4). One variation of the bar sparkline, showing wins and losses, would be an improvement on baseball standings tabulations. In table 6.3, the "L10" and "Streak" columns that are now included in most baseball standings could be replaced by a "Last 10" win/loss sparkline column. The sparkline provides

TABLE 6.2

Reported Crimes and Arrests, New York City, 2001 - 10

	2001	2009	2010	10-year Trend	% change 2001-10	2009-10
Index Crimes:	264,225	188,357	188,104		-29%	-0%
Violent Crimes:	68,737	46,357	48,489		-29%	+5%
Murder	649	471	536		-17%	+14%
Forcible Rape	1,533	832	1,036		-32%	+25%
Robbery	28,206	18,597	19,608		-30%	+5%
Agg. Assault	38,349	26,457	27,309		-29%	+3%
Property Crimes:	195,488	142,000	139,615		-29%	-2%
Burglary	31,564	18,780	17,926		-43%	-5%
Larceny	133,928	112,526	111,370		-17%	-1%
MV Theft	29,996	10,694	10,319		-66%	-4%
Adult Arrests:	298,654	341,003	343,308		+15%	+1%
Felony:	104,158	95,599	92,139		-12%	-4%
Drug	30,289	25,960	22,793		-25%	-12%
Violent	33,802	27,271	27,122		-20%	-1%
DWI	637	724	628		-1%	-13%
Other	39,430	41,644	41,596		+5%	-0%
Misdemeanor:	194,496	245,404	251,169		+29%	+2%
Drug	79,902	82,735	83,298		+4%	+1%
DWI	3,452	8,803	8,218		+138%	-7%
Property	50,451	77,516	81,810		+62%	+6%
Other	60,691	76,350	77,843		+28%	+2%
Adult arrests / *Index crimes*	1.1	1.8	1.8		+61%	+1%
Felony arrests / *violent crimes*	1.5	2.1	1.9		+25%	-8%

Source: New York State Division of Criminal Justice Services

TABLE 6.3

Major League Baseball: 2011 Final Standings

	W	L	PCT	GB	L10	Streak	Last 10
				American League East			
New York	97	65	.599	--	5-5	L4	
Tampa Bay	91	71	.562	6.0	6-4	W5	
Boston	90	72	.556	7.0	3-7	L1	
Toronto	81	81	.500	16.0	4-6	W1	
Baltimore	69	93	.426	22.0	6-4	W1	

Source: MLB.com

a visual display of more information than the two columns combined. Here you can see just how the Tampa Bay Rays overtook the Boston Red Sox to capture the playoff wildcard spot. The Red Sox collapse occurred despite the contributions of the team's senior advisor on baseball operations (Bill James, the founding father of sabermetrics) and despite having egregiously expanded their payroll in a misguided attempt to purchase a championship.

One other form of combining tabular display with graphical content is the databar (included in the 2010 version of Excel). We see in table 6.4 that the United States is ranked 13th in terms of the current (2006) college graduation rate and stands even lower in awarded degrees in mathematics and science fields.

When Graphic Design Goes Badly

To see what happens when the basic rules of data presentation are violated, consider figure 6.19a, taken from Robert Putnam's *Bowling Alone* (where it was labeled figure 47), a work that contains many good and bad examples of graphical data display (and, unfortunately, no tables at all).[20] In just one chart, Putnam violates five basic principles of data display: the chart does not depict meaningful data, the data it does depict are ambiguous, the graphical elements distort the data, the design is seriously inefficient, and the chart is not self-explanatory.

Of the shortcomings, let us consider inefficiency first: the first thing you notice about the chart is the 3-D effect—actually, a double-3-D effect. On both efficiency and truthfulness grounds, this is unfortunate; the 3-D effect is unnecessary and in this case serves to distort the visual representation of the data. Had not the data labels been shown on the top of each bar,

TABLE 6.4
Bachelors Degrees, OECD Nations, 2008

| | Graduation rate* | | % in Math, Science |
	All degrees	Rank /22	and Engineering
Finland	47.5	4	13.8
Sweden	40.6	9	10.6
Australia	49.8	3	10.6
Poland	47.3	5	10.2
New Zealand	51.9	2	10.0
United Kingdom	39.0	12	9.8
Iceland	62.8	1	9.2
Italy	39.4	10	9.2
Portugal	32.9	15	8.4
Spain	32.9	16	8.0
Czech Rep.	29.0	20	7.8
Slovak Rep.	34.6	14	7.3
Denmark	44.6	6	7.2
Ireland	39.1	11	6.9
Switzerland	29.8	19	6.8
Austria	21.5	21	6.3
Netherlands	43.0	7	6.3
United States	**35.5**	**13**	**5.8**
Germany	21.2	22	5.8
Norway	42.6	8	5.6
Canada	30.6	17	5.2
Hungary	30.3	18	4.2

*degrees awarded / population at typical graduation age
Source: *Digest of Education Statistics, 2009*

it would not be readily apparent that bar A is in fact taller than bar F, or that C is the same size as B. In addition, the chart suffers from "numbering inefficiency": the chart uses thirteen numbers to represent just six data points.

The rotation of the 3-D graphic distorts the size of the bars. Bar A, which represents a number (31 percent) only 6 percent larger than the number represented by bar F (29 percent), is at least 20 percent larger than bar F. Eliminating the 3-D, as shown in figure 6.19b, offers a more exact representation of the data with a lot less ink.

But there are still problems with this chart. There are two instances of ambiguous data in Putnam's chart. If one looks at the chart quickly, the first impression one would get is that only 11 percent of women who work full-time do so for reasons of personal satisfaction. But that is not the case. Look at the

Figure 6.19a. Working by Choice and by Necessity among American Women, 1978–1999.

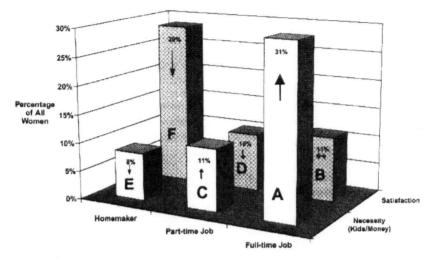

Source: DDB Needham Life Style survey archive, 1978, 1980–1999. Reprinted with permission of Simon and Schuster Adult Publishing Group from *Bowling Alone: the Collapse and Revival of American Community* by Robert D. Putnam. Copyright 2000 by Robert D. Putnam.

y axis title, or notice that the percentages represented by all six bars add up to 100. Of all the women in the survey, 11 percent were in the single category of "employed full-time for reasons of personal satisfaction." This is resolved in Putnam's text, where he explains that bar E is the percentage of all women who are homemakers out of concern for their kids, while bar A is the percentage of all women who are working full-time because they need the money.

The second ambiguity has to do with the part-time category. If women are working part-time for personal satisfaction, does this mean they are not

Figure 6.19b. Reasons Women Work or Stay at Home, 1978–1999.

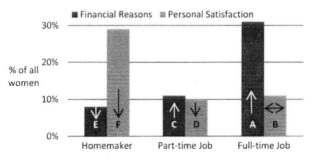

working full-time for personal satisfaction or are they working for personal satisfaction?

Still, we have to ask, "What does this chart mean?" In particular, what data do the arrows on the bars represent?

A critical standard of good charting is that the chart should be self-explanatory. Problems with this chart become apparent to the reader as soon as one encounters Putnam's page and a half of accompanying text devoted to explaining what the elements of the chart represent, not to explaining the significance of the data. A careful reading of the text tells us that Putnam would have us draw three conclusions from this chart:

- Over time (the 1980s and 1990s), more women are working.
- They are doing so less for reasons of personal satisfaction and more out of necessity (i.e., to earn money).
- Correspondingly, there has been a significant decline in the number of women who choose to be homemakers for reasons of personal satisfaction.

These three conclusions are directly relevant to Putnam's general thesis: that over time there has been a decline in social capital (adults are spending less time raising children and developing the social capital of future generations), driven in part by the demands of the expanding workforce. Note that although the conclusions are based on changes over time and the chart title references "1978–1999," nothing in the chart allows for a comparison at two different time points.

Based on the textual discussion that Putnam offers, it becomes clear that the most meaningful data are represented in the chart, not by the height of the bars, but by the direction of the arrows on the bars. Although most of the data analysis in *Bowling Alone* is time series data, in this case Putnam averages twenty-one years of data down to single data points represented by the chart's bars, with the time series change represented by arrows. Thus, the most meaningful comparison in the chart—the comparison that supports the conclusion that Putnam seeks to draw from the data—is not that bar A is higher than bars B or F, but that the arrow for bar A is going up, while the arrow for bar F is going down. The height of the bars is irrelevant to any conclusion Putnam draws from the data.

The crucial comparison is made directly in the revised figure 6.19c, based on the data presented in the textual discussion. Moreover, it directly illustrates several points that neither the text nor the original chart made clear: In 1978, a plurality of women was homemakers who did so out

Figure 6.19c. Reasons Women Work or Stay at Home, 1978–1999.

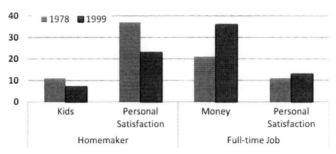

of personal satisfaction. In 1999, the plurality of women was those who worked full-time for financial reasons.

Figure 6.19c also eliminates the ambiguous part-time category and clarifies that "necessity" refers to "kids" in the case of homemakers and to "money" in the case of full-time workers.

NOTES ON MICROSOFT EXCEL CHARTING

All of the charts shown in this book were prepared using the 2010 version of the Microsoft Excel spreadsheet program and some free, downloadable add-ins to the Excel charting software. The 2010 version includes some improvements over the earlier 2003 and 2007 versions, and features of some of the charts take advantage of those improvements. Several of the time series charts use wider lines than were possible in Excel 2003, and the log-scaling features, shown in figures 3.21, 3.23, and 3.26, are not easily replicated in the older version. The two most significant 2011 features are sparklines and databars (horizontal bars), which allow one to include graphical features in the spreadsheet tables (the databars in the 2007 version of Excel do not display well). Table 6.1 also uses icon sets, a new graphical feature. One of the most useful features in the newer versions of Excel, although it cannot be demonstrated in print, is the "format as a table" option, which allows one to sort a table by clicking on the column headings.

Two charting applications should have been included in the newer version of Excel but were not. Boxplots are not a predefined Excel chart option and require some complicated work-arounds. Fortunately, Jon Peltier has created a downloadable Box and Whisker Chart utility that automates the boxplotting process.[21] Most disappointing, the two most recent versions of Excel (2007 and 2010) did not include the chart labeling features necessary to include the country names on the scatterplots in figure 6.15. Several chart labeling macros and add-ins are available on the Internet that add this functionality to the Excel software. The one used here was John Walkenbach's J-Walk Chart Tools.[22] A freeware version (XY Chart Labeler) is available at the Application Professionals website.[23] The labeling feature was also used in some of the other charts to control the placement of notations and to control the spacing of the x axis labels (as in figures 1.2 and 9.8).

All the spreadsheets containing the charts and data shown in this book, with links to the original sources and some advice on using the Excel charting software, are available on the Just Plain Data Analysis website at pol .illinoisstate.edu/jpda/.

**RECOMMENDED READING ON
CHARTING AND GRAPHIC DESIGN**

Cleveland, William S. *Visualizing Data.* Summit, NJ: Hobart Press, 1993.

———. *The Elements of Graphing Data.* Summit, NJ: Hobart Press, 1994.

Few, Stephen. *Show Me the Numbers: Designing Tables and Graphs to Enlighten.* Oakland, CA: Analytics Press, 2004.

———. *Now You See It: Simple Visualization Techniques for Quantitative Analysis.* Oakland, CA: Analytics Press, 2009.

Jones, Gerald E. *How to Lie With Charts.* N.p.: iUniverse.com, 2000.

Kosslyn, Stephen M. *Elements of Graph Design.* New York: Freeman, 1994.

Miller, Jane E. "Creating Effective Charts." In *The Chicago Guide to Writing about Numbers,* chap. 7. Chicago: University of Chicago Press, 2004.

Tufte, Edward R. *The Visual Display of Quantitative Information.* Cheshire, CT: Graphics Press, 1983.

———. *Visual Explanations—Images and Quantities, Evidence and Narrative.* Cheshire, CT: Graphics Press, 1997.

Wainer, Howard. *Visual Revelations: Graphical Tales of Fate and Deception from Napoleon Bonaparte to Ross Perot.* Mahwah, NJ: Lawrence Erlbaum, 1997.

———. *Graphic Discovery.* Princeton, NJ: Princeton University Press, 2005.

———. *Picturing the Uncertain World: How to Understand, Communicate, and Control Uncertainty through Graphical Display.* Princeton, NJ: Princeton University Press, 2009.

Walkenbach, John. *Excel Charts.* New York: Wiley, 2002.

Wallgren, Anders, Britt Wallgren, Rolf Persson, et al. *Graphing Statistics and Data.* Thousand Oaks, CA: Sage Publications, 1996.

Wong, Dona M. *The Wall Street Journal Guide to Information Graphics: The Dos and Don'ts of Presenting Data, Facts, and Figures.* New York: Norton, 2010.

Notes

1. Darrell Huff, *How to Lie with Statistics* (New York: Norton, 1993).

2. Edward Tufte, *The Visual Display of Quantitative Information* (Cheshire, CT: Graphics Press, 1983).

3. "No Politician Left Behind," *Wall Street Journal*, February 15, 2004.

4. If you re-read the section on the closing the gap fallacy, you might notice that I've cheated here. The percentage change in those scoring above 200 is 23%, but the change in the percentage below 200 is –16%.

5. Dona M. Wong, *The Wall Street Journal Guide to Information Graphics: The Dos and Don'ts of Presenting Data, Facts, and Figures* (New York: Norton, 2010).

6. William Strunk and E. B. White, *The Elements of Style* (New York: Macmillan, 1972), 25.

7. Clarke E. Cochran, Lawrence C. Mayer, T. R. Carr, et al., *American Public Policy: An Introduction*, 10th ed. (Boston: Wadsworth, 2012), 98.

8. "Privatisation," *The Economist*, December 21, 1985, 72.

9. Illinois Board of Higher Education, *Illinois Higher Education Annual Report* (Springfield: Illinois Board of Higher Education, July 2002), 29.

10. Jane E. Miller, *The Chicago Guide to Writing about Numbers* (Chicago: University of Chicago Press, 2004), 160.

11. Howard Wainer, *Visual Revelations: Graphical Tales of Fate and Deception from Napoleon Bonaparte to Ross Perot* (Mahwah, NJ: Lawrence Erlbaum, 1997), 27.

12. Wong, *The Wall Street Journal Guide to Information Graphics*, 64–65.

13. Norman H. Nie, Sidney Verba, and John R. Petrocik, *The Changing American Voter* (Cambridge, MA: Harvard University Press, 1979).

14. Public Agenda, "Public Agenda for Citizens," http://www.publicagenda.org/citizen/issueguides/federal-budget (accessed July 2009).

15. Clarke E. Cochran et al., *American Public Policy*, 119.

16. Florida Department of Law Enforcement, "UCR Officer Data," at http://www.fdle.state.fl.us/Content/FSAC/Data—Statistics-%281%29/UCR-Officer-Data/UCR-Officer-Data.aspx (accessed July 1, 2011).

17. "Gapminder World," at http://www.gapminder.org (accessed July 8, 2011).

18. The Google Public Data Explorer at http://www.google.com/publicdata (accessed October 8, 2011).

19. Edward Tufte, *Beautiful Evidence* (Cheshire, CT: Graphics Press, 2006), 7–25.

20. Robert D. Putnam, *Bowling Alone* (New York: Simon & Schuster, 2000).

21. Jon Peltier, "Box and Whisker Plots," Peltier Technical Services, Inc., at http://peltiertech.com/Excel/Charts/BoxWhisker.html.

22. John Walkenbach, "J-Walk Chart Tools," at http://www.jwalk.com/ss/excel/files/charttools.htm.

23. Application Professionals, "XY Chart Labeler," at http://www.appspro.com/Utilities/ChartLabeler.htm (accessed July 1, 2011).

CHAPTER 7

Voting and Elections

A low voter turnout is an indication of fewer people going to
the polls.

—DAN QUAYLE

V OTER TURNOUT, the percentage of a population that turns out to vote,
  is a commonly used indicator of the health of a society's democracy and
the level of civic engagement in public affairs. High rates of voter turnout are
often cited as an indicator of public confidence in democratic institutions.
In December of 2005, for example, the Bush administration enthusiastically
trumpeted the 80 percent turnout (as a percentage of registered voters) in Iraq's
first parliamentary elections as a measure of popular support for the democratic process.[1] Political commentators often cite voter turnout as an indicator
of either the strength of a society's political culture or the quality of its political institutions. An informed and engaged citizenry that embraces shared values and common interests is more likely to participate in elections. A political
system that is responsive to voter interests, offers voters meaningful choices in
contested elections, and welcomes open and broad-based political participation
offers citizens greater incentives to participate in elections.

Low voter turnout and bad government go hand in hand, as we saw in
the relationship between voter turnout and political corruption in chapter
3 (figure 3.2). Entrenched political machines often flourish in a low-turnout
political environment, where they can mobilize cadres of supporters and
clients to assure safe reelection. Barriers to voting often serve the interests
of incumbent politicians, whose positions are at greater risk when new voters turn out at the polls.

For many who study voting behavior, variations in the rate of voter
turnout across various social and demographic groups are a critical aspect
of a nation's democratic culture. Who participates in elections often deter-
mines who benefits from the election outcomes. Because the elderly, the
wealthy, and the better educated generally have higher rates of voting,

increasing voter turnout usually requires increasing the participation of the young, poor, and less educated voters. In theory, political systems with low voter turnout will be less responsive to the needs of society's "have nots" and more responsive to the interests of those with power.[2]

INTERNATIONAL VOTER TURNOUT

Voter turnout is one of many social indicators on which the United States ranks near the bottom among the world's developed democracies. In recent national elections (table 7.1), only three OECD nations averaged a lower voter turnout than the United States. U.S. turnout fares poorly even in comparison to many nondemocratic nations. Among the 140 countries holding two or more elections between 1948 and 1998, U.S. voter turnout ranked 114.[3]

For some, the embarrassing low American voter turnout reflects systemic flaws in American culture. Robert Putnam argues that low and declining voter turnout is the "canary in the mining pit" and is indicative of a general lack of civic engagement.[4] Often, low turnout is linked to pervasive American individualism and public distrust of government. Others argue that Americans have been alienated and turned off by politics and blame nasty election campaigning, talk radio and cable news, and divisively partisan incumbent politicians. Still others argue that low voter turnout is a consequence of an undemocratic election and political system that goes out of its way to make voting, particularly poor-and-minority voting, more difficult.[5]

Russell J. Dalton, however, challenges what he calls the "myth of the disengaged American voter."[6] First, consider that Americans actually vote much more often than the citizens of other democracies; no other democracy offers its citizens as many opportunities to vote. The United States holds congressional elections every two years, about twice as often as most parliamentary democracies. Many states also conduct statewide elections during odd-numbered years, and some schedule local elections separately from statewide elections. Almost all of these elections involve both a primary and general election. Few countries hold primary elections, and rarer still is the practice of several American states of holding "open" primaries, permitting nonmembers of political parties to participate.

In addition, the number of offices Americans vote for is truly exceptional. In 2009, French president Nicolas Sarkozy proposed a reform of his country's "notoriously complex system of local government" by cutting back the number of elected local officials from six thousand to three thousand.[7] In contrast, the state of Illinois has over forty thousand local elected officials.[8] The state holds elections for county legislators, judges, treasurers,

TABLE 7.1

Voter Turnout in the Last Three National Elections, OECD Nations

	Proportional representation	Turnout: last 3 national elections			Average
Belgium	yes	86	86	93	88
Iceland	yes	89	85	85	86
Denmark	yes	84	81	83	83
Greece	yes	88	80	79	82
Italy	yes	85	82	79	82
Australia	no	82	83	81	82
Sweden	yes	78	81	83	80
Spain	yes	74	80	78	77
New Zealand	yes	72	79	78	77
Turkey	yes	80	74	74	76
Korea	yes	92	71	64	76
Austria	yes	77	73	76	75
Netherlands	yes	78	77	71	75
Norway	yes	74	77	75	75
France	n\a	72	70	77	73
Germany	yes	73	72	65	70
Finland	yes	70	68	70	69
Czech Republic	yes	59	65	78	68
Ireland	yes	67	69	64	67
Portugal	yes	69	66	64	67
Slovenia	yes	72	61	65	66
Japan	yes	59	67	69	65
Chile	yes	67	64	60	63
Mexico	n\a	66	60	63	63
Slovakia	yes	72	56	58	62
United Kingdom	no	58	58	61	59
Poland	n\a	63	51	55	56
Luxembourg	yes	57	57	53	56
Canada	no	58	54	54	55
UNITED STATES	**no**	**47**	**57**	**57**	**54**
Estonia	yes	48	53	55	52
Hungary	yes	55	41	59	52
Switzerland	yes	35	37	40	37

*Poland, Mexico, France: presidential only elections

Source: International Institute for Democracy and Electoral Assistance

clerks, recorders, assessors, and coroners. Within each county, often-overlapping city, town, township, fire protection districts, water reclamation districts, sanitary districts, library districts, community college districts, and school districts also have elective assemblies, boards, and executive offices. In Cook County, Illinois, 516 presidents, vice presidents, treasurers, and commissioners are elected to the governing boards of the 102 local park districts.

We should also consider that voting is not the only means of citizen participation. The Comparative Study of Electoral Systems (CSES) project provides data obtained from a common module of questions asked in surveys conducted just after the national elections held in most OECD nations, and several others. Dalton cites these data to argue that Americans, on a wide variety of CSES measures of civic and electoral participation, consistently surpass the citizens of most other nations.[9] When asked if they have contacted government officials or worked with others on a political issue, Americans ranked among the most engaged in political affairs (figure 7.1). Interestingly, the six English-speaking countries have the highest rates of citizens contacting government officials.

Figure 7.1. Civic Participation in 21 OECD Nations, 2004.

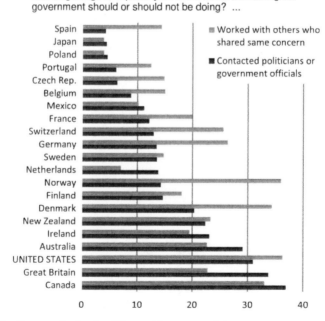

Source: The Comparative Study of Electoral Systems, module 2.

A separate set of national surveys conducted in 2004 by the International Social Survey Programme asked respondents whether they had participated in each of seven political activities over the previous year. Of the thirty-nine nations surveyed, the United States scored in the top quartile on most of the items and above the median on all seven (figure 7.2).

If American political culture does not account for the low voter turnout, the more likely explanations would have to do with some of the peculiar aspects of American electoral systems. Of the OECD nations shown in table 7.1, only five (Great Britain, France, Australia, Canada, and the United States) use single-member legislative districts for national legislative elections. The others use some form of proportional representation, a system that provides minor parties a better chance at gaining legislative seats, thus encouraging voters to turn out for parties that otherwise would stand little chance of gaining a plurality of the vote. Of the five single-member-district countries, only Australia has a record of high voter turnout, perhaps because it is one of only three countries that enforces a compulsory voting law. Because single-member districts are less likely to have close elections, voters have less reason to go to the polls. This is exacerbated in most American states, and not in the other countries using single member districts, by political gerrymandering—the process by which elected officials choose their voters rather than the other way around. Although the past two presidential elections have been very close contests, the American Electoral College presidential candidates spend their time and resources on the closely contested "battleground" states, leaving most of the country uncontested.

The U.S. system of voter registration, with most states requiring that voters register at least thirty days before the election, is also a significant

Figure 7.2. Participation Rates in Political Activities in the Past Year (2004): United States and 38 Nations.

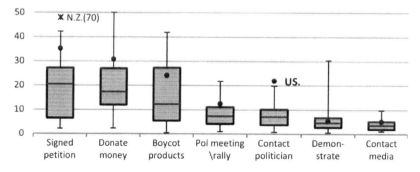

Source: International Social Survey Programme, 39 Nation Citizenship Survey.

impediment to voting. In effect, many European and Latin American countries have an automatic system of voter registration using some form of universal "national registry."[10] Under proportional representation, in which legislators are selected based on national vote totals, voters do not have to register with local election authorities. Moreover, the United States is one of very few countries to not hold elections on weekends or national holidays, making it difficult for many workers and commuters to go to the polls.

One unique feature of the American election system that would be expected to result in higher voter turnout—the enormous sums of money spent on election campaign advertisement—does not seem to help.

MEASURING U.S. VOTER TURNOUT

One would think that calculating a statistic like voter turnout would be straightforward. The statistic is simple enough: the percentage of people who voted. When it comes to actually constructing the indicator, however, we find that there are consequential choices to be made in defining both the numerator and the denominator.

With the international data shown in table 7.1, and with the most commonly cited U.S. turnout measure, the numerator count is not the number of people who "turned out" to vote, but the number of valid votes cast for the highest office on the ballot. This is done partly because many countries, and some states, only count the number of valid votes even if a voter leaves the choice for some offices blank. Some voters, however, may not vote for the highest office and, as Americans learned in the 2000 election, the number of valid votes cast can be less than the number of votes people intended to cast.

Most commonly, the voting age population is used as the divisor. In the 2008 U.S. election, 131 million votes were cast for president, 57 percent of the voting age population of 230 million (the lower trend in figure 7.3). Although by this measure the 2008 turnout represented a significant improvement over the past three elections, U.S. voter turnout since World War II has generally decreased.

Although there are some uncounted votes, the "votes cast" turnout statistics, based on actual election records, can represent a reliable measure of voter turnout for the population as a whole. These data, however, are often not of much use to researchers who wish to investigate who voted and why. Because the voting is by secret ballot, the votes-cast data cannot tell us whether women, blacks, evangelical Protestants, conservatives, or any other group other than those defined by electoral boundaries, voted in high or low numbers. To analyze turnout among different parts of the electorate, we have to rely on surveys.

Figure 7.3. Three Measures of Voter Turnout.

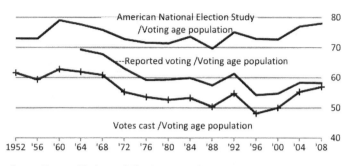

Sources: Census Bureau, Voting and Elections; US Elections Project;
ANES Guide to Public Opinion and Electoral Behavior.

Two different surveys provide the evidence for most of the research on American voting behavior. The *American National Election Studies* (ANES), conducted for presidential and congressional elections since 1948, is based on face-to-face, pre- and postelection interviews, usually of over 1,400 respondents. The ANES surveys have been the key data for most of the political science research on American voting behavior, but as we see in figure 7.3 (the upper trend), the ANES dramatically and increasingly overestimates the percentage of Americans who vote. Although the survey has a sampling error of only about 3 percent; 78 percent of ANES respondents reported voting in 2008, more than 20 percentage points higher than the rate based on the votes cast.

There are many reasons for this discrepancy. First is a phenomenon known as the Hawthorne effect: because respondents know they are being studied, their behavior changes. The ANES surveys the same respondents both before and after the election, asking them whether and for whom they voted in the postelection survey. Thus, the preelection interview may taint the postelection turnout data: Sitting through an hour-long preelection interview about political issues may make people more likely to vote. Second, although the ANES is much more rigorous than most election polls in its efforts to contact respondents, the survey suffers from an increasing nonresponse rate.[11] The discrepancy between votes-cast turnout numbers and the ANES turnout numbers has increased over the years as the response rate to the postelection survey has dropped from the mid-70 percent range to the low 50 percent range. It is reasonable to speculate that those least likely to participate in election surveys are also least likely to vote.

The ANES survey may also suffer from a sample-mortality effect. Having sat through the preelection survey, those respondents least interested in politics and least likely to vote may have been most unwilling to participate in the second interview. And those who said that they would vote in the preelection survey but did not may not want to be asked about it in the postelection survey.

The final reason for the high ANES turnout rates is the most discouraging of all: People lie. It's not that they forget; the postelection interviews are conducted in the month following the election. We know they lie, and we even know who the liars are because the ANES has cross-checked the respondents' answers with their actual voting records. Since 1972, the ANES validated-voter data have consistently indicated that over 40 percent of the people who had not actually voted said that they had. Southern whites, African Americans, Latinos, college-educated persons, and (this is most discouraging) frequent churchgoers are among those most likely to "overreport" voting.[12]

The dirty little secret of voting behavior research is that this is the only question that has been cross-checked; we do not know how many people lied in response to the other questions that the interviewers asked. Separate analyses have shown that the rates of church attendance reported in major national surveys are about twice that of actual church attendance, suggesting that the relationship between churchgoing and voting may have something to do with the same people lying on both questions.[13] It should be a bumper sticker: Statistics don't lie, people do!

The U.S. Census Bureau conducts the second commonly used voting behavior survey, the November *Current Population Survey*, following each congressional election. The Census "reported voting" turnout estimates, although higher than the votes-cast estimates, are generally more reliable than the ANES figures. In recent elections, the Census turnout data have been based on phone and face-to-face interviews with over 60,000 adults; the November 2000 survey had a response rate of 87 percent compared to the ANES's 52 percent.[14] The Census survey allows for demographic analyses of voter turnout, but it lacks party affiliation and political attitudinal questions that inform much of the voting behavior research done with ANES data. While the ANES turnout rate increasingly diverges from the actual votes-cast rate, the Census Bureau's reported-voting rate is getting closer (the middle line in figure 7.3). For the 2008 election, the 58.2 percent reported-voting turnout rate was just over a percentage point higher than the votes-cast rate.[15] Perhaps Americans are becoming less likely to lie to their government. If only it were the other way around.

Using the Census reported-voting turnout numbers, we see that the general decline in voter turnout has occurred primarily among the youngest voters (figure 7.4). Those over age sixty-five have actually increased their voting rates and, because the size of the elderly population is increasing faster than the rest of the population, their voting power has increased dramatically.

Figure 7.4. Reported Voter Turnout (/voting age population) by Age, 1964–2008.

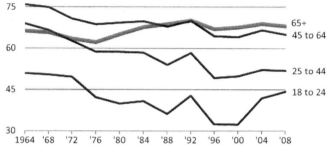

*Voting age population.
Source: Census Bureau, Voting and Registration.

Nevertheless, in the 2004 and 2008 elections, the pattern may have reversed itself, as the youngest voters showed the greatest increase in turnout.

Education has a strong positive correlation with voter turnout (figure 7.5), even though the elderly, who have the highest turnout rates, generally have lower levels of educational attainment. Although the United States' sorry history of denying African Americans the vote underlies much of the conflict over voting rights, black voter turnout is only marginally less than that of whites, particularly when we consider differences in education. Reported white turnout was 66 percent in the 2008 election compared to 65 percent for blacks, but at each level of educational attainment less than a college degree, blacks were actually more likely to vote. In addition, racial differences in income and age, both positively correlated with voting, tend to result in lower black turnout. Asian and Hispanic voter turnout, however,

Figure 7.5. Reported Voter Turnout, by Race and Education, 2008 (% of voting age citizens).

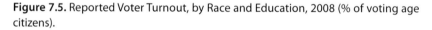

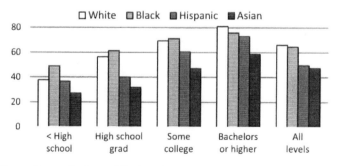

Source: Census Bureau, Voting and Registration, 2008.

is dramatically lower even when "voting age citizens," rather than voting age population, is used as the turnout rate denominator.

Political commentary about turned-off voters reached its peak after the 1996 election, when the votes-cast measure of voter turnout fell below 50 percent. In 2001, however, political scientist Michael McDonald compiled new data suggesting that the talk about the vanishing American voter was "a myth."[16] McDonald's analysis called attention to the denominator in the voting turnout statistic—*voting age population*—and argued that we should instead use the *voting eligible population*. During recent elections, an increasing percentage of the American voting age population has not been eligible to vote. This is primarily because of increasing immigration: both legal and nonlegal noncitizen residents are counted in the Census Bureau voting age population figures. In addition, in all but two states, prisoners are not allowed to vote, and in twelve states even ex-felons are disenfranchised. Because the percentage of the American population that is either incarcerated or has ex-felon status has risen dramatically since the 1980s, an increasing percentage of the voting age population cannot vote. The Sentencing Project, an advocacy organization, estimates that felony disenfranchisement laws have disenfranchised 13 percent of all black males.[17]

Using McDonald's votes cast as a percentage of the voting eligible population (figure 7.6) as our measure of turnout, we see no general decline in voter turnout since 1972, when eighteen-year-olds were given the franchise. An even more dramatic increase can be seen over the past three elections. In 2008, over 62 percent of voter-eligible Americans voted, the highest turnout rate since the passage of the Voting Rights Act in 1965.

So which is the better measure of voter turnout? It depends on just what you are trying to measure. For McDonald, voter turnout is a measure of civic engagement. McDonald's use of the voting eligible population is

Figure 7.6. Turnout: Voting Age vs. Voting Eligible Population Divisors.

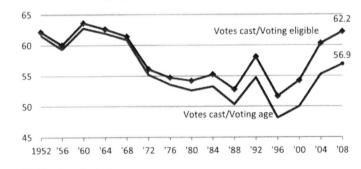

Sources: US Elections Project.

appropriate when he is addressing arguments having to do with how well the election process inspires potential voters to participate in the elections.

But if you look at voter turnout as a measure of how democratic a society is, the traditional "votes cast as a percentage of voting age population" numbers have greater validity. Although voting-eligible turnout is increasing and at a longtime high, this is due in part to the degree that the nation has become less democratic. Voter turnout is as high as it is because so many young black males (unlikely voters to begin with) have been put in jail and, in many states, denied the right to vote for the rest of their lives, and because so many of our nation's poor are not citizens. If all young voters (the age group least likely to vote) were incarcerated and all the poor (the economic group least likely to vote) were declared noncitizens, the American voting eligible turnout rate would be among the highest in the world, but the United States would not be a more democratic society.

Analyzing a Relationship: Election Day Registration

A common explanation for low American voter turnout is that American election rules generally create significant barriers to voting. Democratic partisans often allege that these barriers are intentional and designed to make it more difficult for new voters and poor voters to participate in elections. Defenders of these election rules argue that they are designed to preserve the integrity of elections and to discourage voter fraud.

State laws that are allegedly designed to restrict voting include the disenfranchisement of felons, ranging from prohibitions on prisoners voting (in all but two states) to lifetime prohibitions on felons voting in ten states, which affect between three million and five million persons, half of them no longer serving time in jail or prison.[18] After Republicans captured 12 state legislatures (for a total of 26) in the 2010 election, 6 states passed laws requiring photo IDs for voting, bringing the total to 17, and similar legislation is under consideration in several other states.[19] Opponents of the legislation argue that poor and minority voters are least likely to have the required photo IDs and that their voting participation will be impaired. College students who vote at their campus address will be particularly affected by these laws unless they have acquired a new driver's license or state-issued photo ID.

Other states have enacted laws intended to facilitate voting. Oregon, beginning in 1998, and Washington, starting in 2011, now conduct their elections entirely with mail ballots. Other states have begun to implement early voting, sometimes called "no-excuse absentee voting." In the 2008 presidential election, 57 percent of North Carolina's voters took advantage of the state's combination of early voting and same-day registration to vote in the month before Election Day. The state's turnout increased by almost 11 percent over 2004, the highest increase in the nation.[20]

One of the alleged barriers to voter participation is the requirement of most states that voters register for elections, usually one month before Election Day. Ten American states allow voters to register on Election Day when they show up to vote. Of these, North Dakota does not require any voter registration. Three states—Idaho, New Hampshire, and Wyoming—have allowed Election Day registration since 1996, and Maine, Minnesota, and Wisconsin since at least 1980. Iowa, Montana, and North Carolina allowed Election Day registration for the first time in a presidential election in 2008.

Many credit Jesse Ventura's election as governor of Minnesota in 1998 to the state's Election Day registration (EDR) procedure. Ventura was the "Reform Party" candidate and well behind in the polls through most of the election campaign. But in the closing weeks of the campaign, after the final gubernatorial debate, Ventura's campaign caught fire, attracting new and younger voters to the polls, many of whom might not have been able to vote had standard registration policies been in effect.

One of the groups advocating Election Day registration is *Demos*, a non-partisan public policy research and advocacy organization. *Demos* distributes a four-page advocacy toolkit that features, on its cover, two bar charts indicating the voter turnout in EDR states (Idaho, Maine, Minnesota, New Hampshire, Wisconsin, and Wyoming) and non-EDR states in the 2000 and 2004 presidential elections. Demos summarizes the data:

> EDR significantly increases the opportunity to cast a vote and participate in American democracy. Six states—Idaho, Maine, Minnesota, New Hampshire, Wisconsin, and Wyoming—offered EDR in the 2004 presidential election. These states boasted, on average, voter turnout that was 12 percentage points higher than in non-EDR states, and reported few problems with fraud, costs, or administrative complexity.[21]

For the 2000 election, Demos reports that EDR states had a 68 percent turnout compared to a 59 percent turnout in non-EDR states, a 9-point gap.

Here, Demos states a descriptive conclusion (EDR states have higher turnout) but clearly implies a causal explanation: Election Day registration causes a higher voter turnout. To assess whether this is a reasonable conclusion, we must first examine the reliability and validity of the turnout measures used.

Although the actual turnout measure is not identified in the *Demos* report, the high turnout rates reported indicate that they are using "reported voting," the turnout measure based on the Census Bureau's November survey and voting-age-citizen population as the divisor (table 7.2). In addition, to calculate the average turnout in the EDR and non-EDR states, *Demos* has reported the averages weighted by the population of the states. Because the two EDR states with the highest turnout, Minnesota and Wisconsin, each have a larger population than the other four EDR states combined, the weighted average substantially increases the turnout measure for the EDR states. Using the average-of-the-states turnout reduces the 12-point gap by more than a third.

On the other hand, *Demos* did not include North Dakota, which has no registration requirement, as an EDR state. Including North Dakota's turnout of just over 70 percent in both elections would have increased the EDR average in 2000 but slightly reduced it in 2004. Using "votes cast" as the numerator, "voting-eligible" as the divisor, and including North Dakota as an EDR state, we see (table 7.3) that EDR states maintain a consistently higher turnout than non-EDR states, although the difference has declined as new states have adopted the procedure.

TABLE 7.2
Reported Voter Turnout* in Election Day Registration States. 2000 and 2004

	2000	2004
EDR states:		
Minnesota	69.8	79.2
Wisconsin	70.1	76.6
Maine	70.1	73.1
New Hampshire	66.6	71.5
Wyoming	62.9	66.9
Idaho	56.1	61.6
State average :		
EDR states	65.9	71.5
Non-EDR states	59.9	64.2
Difference		
EDR-(non-EDR)	+6.0	+7.3
Weighted by population:		
EDR states	68.2	75.1
Non-EDR states	59.2	63.2
Difference		
EDR-(non-EDR)	+9.0	+11.9

* of voting age citizen population
Source: Census Bureau, Voting and Registration;
Demos, Election Day Registration Helps America Vote

TABLE 7.3

Voter Turnout* in Election Day Registration States, 1980-'08

EDR states	Election	EDR States	Non-EDR	Difference
ND, ME, MN, WI, OR	1980	67.7	56.0	+11.7
	1984	67.0	56.6	+10.4
ND, ME, MN, WI	1988	65.1	54.9	+10.2
	1992	71.6	60.1	+11.4
ND, ME, MN, WI, ID, NH, WY	1996	61.6	53.0	+8.6
	2000	64.5	55.3	+9.2
	2004	71.0	61.5	+9.5
ND, ME, MN, WI, ID, NH, WY, IA, MT, NC	2008	69.4	62.6	+6.8

* Votes cast/voting eligible population
Source: United States Elections Project

Next, we must consider the possibility that some other factors might account for the relatively higher voter turnout in EDR states. First, it is possible that the EDR states happened to have more contentious elections during these years. These states may have been "battleground states" and targeted by the presidential election campaigns for heavier advertising and get-out-the-vote efforts, or there may have been closely contested gubernatorial or Senate elections.

Also consider that the ten EDR states are unlike the other states in many ways. Nine of the ten EDR states either border Canada or border another EDR state that borders Canada. North Carolina is the exception. Some aspects of the political culture of these states may account for their higher voter turnout.

One measure of a state's political culture is Robert Putnam's Social Capital Index.[22] The index combines thirteen measures[23] of civic engagement relating to participation in community organizations, public affairs, volunteerism, and attitudes of public trust and sociability. The scatterplot in figure 7.7, using the average turnout over four elections—to partially discount the effect of particularly contentious state elections—indicates, first, that social capital is strongly related to Election Day registration laws: All the EDR states, except North Carolina, have above-average social capital scores. There is also a strong positive correlation between social capital and turnout. The key question, however, is whether the EDR states have high turnout because they have high social capital or because of the EDR laws.

Figure 7.7. Social Capital and Voter Turnout (/voting eligible population), Presidential Elections, 1996–2008.

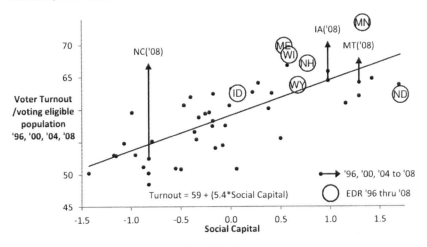

Sources: US Elections Project; Bowling Alone Website.

The evidence in figure 7.7 suggests that high social capital accounts for some, but not all, of the higher turnout in EDR states. Nine of the ten EDR states had voter turnout higher than predicted given their social capital. The three states that began using EDR in the 2008 election saw their turnout increase: In the three elections before 2008, the turnout in these states was at or below what would be expected given their level of social capital; but in 2008, each state moved above the prediction line. Only North Dakota's turnout was lower than would be expected based on social capital score.

Using the formula for the regression line in figure 7.7

$$\text{Voter turnout} = 59 + (5.4 \times \text{Social Capital})$$

we can compare the voter turnout in each of the states to the voter turnout predicted by the state's social capital scores. Idaho, for example, has a social capital score of .1. Thus, its predicted voter turnout would be 59.54 percent (59 + .54). The state's actual turnout was 3 percentage points higher (62.5 percent).

On average, turnout in EDR states is 4.5 percentage points higher than non-EDR turnout after discounting for the effects of social capital (table 7.4). Although this is less than Demos seems to suggest, a 4.5 percentage point increase in turnout rates could easily affect election outcomes.

Even so, social capital is not the only factor that may account for this relationship. A variety of factors peculiar to the ten states or idiosyncratic factors peculiar to each of the states and the three elections may be at work here.

TABLE 7.4

Actual and Predicted Voter Turnout, Election Day Registration States

	Social Capital	Average Turnout '96 thru '08		
		Actual	Predicted**	Difference
North Dakota	1.7	62.3	68.3	-6.0
Minnesota	1.3	73.4	66.2	+7.2
Montana*	1.3	67.5	66.0	+1.5
Iowa*	1.0	70.0	64.3	+5.7
New Hampshire	0.8	67.1	63.2	+3.9
Wyoming	0.7	63.8	62.6	+1.1
Wisconsin	0.6	68.4	62.2	+6.2
Maine	0.5	69.9	61.9	+8.0
Idaho	0.1	62.5	59.5	+3.0
North Carolina*	-0.8	66.7	54.5	+12.2
All EDR states	0.7	67.2	62.9	+4.3
Non-EDR states	-0.2	57.9	58.1	-0.2

* 2008 Turnout

** Predicted Turnout = 59 + (5.4 x Social Capital)

Sources: US Elections Project: Bowling Alone Website

North Carolina's increase in turnout in the 2008 election is the most striking, and a variety of other factors only indirectly related to Election Day registration may account for the increase. The state combined Election Day registration with very lenient early-voting policies. The state has a large black population, and in 2008 it is said that black ministers took advantage of the new policies and brought whole congregations to register and vote after Sunday services.

North Carolina had not been considered a "battleground" state (it last went Democratic in Jimmy Carter's 1976 election) until polls started to show that most early voters were voting for Barack Obama. Obama won North Carolina by a mere 14,000 votes, out of 4 million cast.

Based on the evidence presented here, there is no reason to believe that Election Day registration will result in dramatic voter turnout gains in normal presidential elections. But be aware of the limitations of the evidence. All the data shown here concerned presidential elections. If Election Day registration laws do affect turnout, one might expect that the most dramatic effects would be in nonpresidential elections that usually have lower turnout, such as Ventura's gubernatorial election. Evaluating the effect of the laws on off-year elections would require a far more elaborate analysis, taking into account the differences in the nature of each election campaign.

Nor do we know what effect Election Day registration might have on presidential elections in states with historically low voter turnout. With the exception of North Carolina in 2008, the states that have implemented these laws were high social capital and high turnout states to begin with. Except for the lack of evidence, there is every reason to believe that the laws would have their greatest impact in low social capital and low turnout states. But the phrase "except for the lack of evidence" is a crucial qualification, and we may never know what would happen in the EDR states were Jesse Ventura to run for president.

Notes

1. George W. Bush, "President's Address to the Nation," The White House, Office of the Press Secretary, December 18, 2005, at http://www.whitehouse.gov/news/releases/2005/12/20051218-2.html.

2. V. O. Key Jr., *Southern Politics in State and Nation* (New York: Knopf, 1949).

3. International Institute for Democracy and Electoral Assistance, "Voter Turnout," March 7, 2005, at http://www.idea.int/vt/.

4. Robert D. Putnam, *Bowling Alone: The Collapse and Revival of American Community* (New York: Simon & Schuster, 2000), 35.

5. Frances Fox Piven and Richard A. Cloward, *Why Americans Still Don't Vote, and Why Politicians Want It That Way* (Boston: Beacon, 2000).

6. Russell J. Dalton, "The Myth of the Disengaged American," *Public Opinion Pros,* October 2005, at http://www.publicopinionpros.com/features/2005/oct/dalton.asp.

7. Peggy Hollinger, "Sarkozy Faces Anger in His Own Party," *Financial Times,* October 21, 2009, at http://www.ft.com/cms/s/0/358026c2-be72-11de-b4ab-00144feab49a.html#axzz1ceXd5n00.

8. U.S. Bureau of Census, *2002 Census of Governments,* vol. 2, *Popularly Elected Officials* (June 1995), table 2.

9. Dalton, "The Myth of the Disengaged American."

10. R. Michael Alvarez, "Voter Registration," Caltech/MIT Voting Technology Project, April 30, 2001, at http://www.vote.caltech.edu/media/documents/testimony/050301_Alvarez.pdf.

11. For a debate on the role of response rate, see Barry C. Burden, "Voter Turnout and the National Election Studies," *Political Analysis* 8 (July 2000): 389–98, and Michael P. McDonald, "On the Overreport Bias of the National Election Study Turnout Rate," *Political Analysis* 11 (Spring 2003): 180–86.

12. Robert Bernstein, Anita Chadha, and Robert Montjoy, "Overreporting Voting: Why It Happens and Why It Matters," *Public Opinion Quarterly* 65 (Spring 2001): 22–44.

13. C. Kirk Hadaway, Penny Long Marler, and Mark Chaves, "What the Polls Don't Show: A Closer Look at U.S. Church Attendance," *American Sociological Review* 58(6): 741–52.

14. Benjamin Highton, "Self-Reported versus Proxy-Reported Voter Turnout in the Current Population Survey," *Public Opinion Quarterly* 69 (Spring 2005): 113–23.

15. Part of the difference between the "reported voting" and "votes cast" rates may be due to survey respondents who did not cast valid votes for president and to slightly different definitions of the voting age population.

16. Michael P. McDonald and Samuel Popkin, "The Myth of the Vanishing Voter," *American Political Science Review* 95, no. 4 (2001): 963–74.

17. The Sentencing Project, "Federal Voting Rights for People with Convictions," February 2007, at http://www.sentencingproject.org/Admin/Documents/publications/fd_bs_peoplewithconvictions.pdf.

18. The 3.1 million estimate was obtained from the U.S. Elections Project for the 2008 election, at http://elections.gmu.edu/Turnout_2008G.html. The Sentencing Project (at http://www.sentencingproject.org/template/page.cfm?id=133) estimates the disfranchised population to be 5.3 million.

19. Fredreka Schouten, "More States Require ID to Vote," *USA Today*, June 20, 2011, at http://www.usatoday.com/news/nation/2011-06-19-states-require-voter-ID_n.htm.

20. Nonprofit Voter Engagement Network, "America Goes to the Polls: A Report on Voter Turnout in the 2008 Election," at http://www.nonprofitvote.org/download-document/america-goes-to-the-polls-2008-pdf.htm.

21. Demos, "Election Day Registration Helps America Vote," Summer–Fall 2006, at http://archive.demos.org/pubs/EDR%20Toolkit%20070506.pdf.

22. Putnam, *Bowling Alone,* 288–95.

23. Putnam's Social Capital Index included voter turnout as one of fourteen variables in the index. Here, the index has been recalculated to exclude the turnout measure.

Measuring Educational Achievement

Weighing a hog doesn't make him fatter.
—JOHN EDWARDS, ON THE NO CHILD LEFT BEHIND LAW

FOR THE most part, I find teaching to be a most rewarding profession. If only I didn't have to grade those papers and exams. One would think that teachers would be pleased if someone offered to prepare and grade their students' exams for them. This has actually happened for our nation's public school teachers. Since 2005, state departments of education have developed, administered, and graded standardized tests in reading, writing, science, and mathematics annually to almost every student in grades three through eight and eleven. But many teachers and school officials are not happy, primarily because the tests are not used to grade the students so much as they are used to grade the schools, the school administrators, and the teachers. Just as students receive grades on their report cards, states now send school district report cards to parents, reporting each school's and school district's scores on the tests. As a result, many teachers and administrators who have spent years listening to their students' excuses for poor test performance with bemused incredulity are now developing explanations of their own.

Much of the current effort to develop national standards for measuring student performance grew out of the 1983 report *A Nation at Risk*, prepared by the National Commission on Excellence in Education. The report's opening sentences were meant to elicit alarm reminiscent of the reaction to the Soviet Union's launch of Sputnik in 1957:

> Our Nation is at risk. Our once unchallenged preeminence in commerce, industry, science, and technological innovation is being overtaken by competitors throughout the world.[1]

Among the evidence cited in support of the commission's conclusions were the findings of several international measures of student learning:

> International comparisons of student achievement, completed a decade ago, reveal that on 19 academic tests American students were never first or second and, in comparison with other industrialized nations, were last seven times.[2]

The findings went against the conventional wisdom. The American economy was the strongest in the world due in large part to advances in science and technology. America had responded to the Sputnik challenge by landing a man on the moon. In medicine, computers, communications, and industrial technology, the United States was the unchallenged world leader. The number of patents issued and Nobel prizes won far surpassed the rest of the world. The reasons for the success, it was believed, were deeply embedded in American culture and politics. While other nations' governments pursued socialist and welfare state social policies, the United States promoted equality of opportunity by investing in education. The United States (and Germany) had led the world in developing a universal public education system. American higher education enrollment surpassed that of all other nations, and the prestige of U.S. colleges and universities was unquestioned.

INTERNATIONAL EDUCATION INDICATORS

Of the nineteen measures referred to in the *Nation at Risk* report, the most comprehensive and reliable data were obtained from cross-national tests developed by the International Education Association (IEA): the First International Mathematics Study, conducted in the 1960s, and the First International Science Study, conducted in the late 1960s and early 1970s. The results, shown in table 8.1, were not good: The United States ranked near the bottom on most tests, especially for students in the higher grades.

In subsequent years, other international tests were developed, standards for the consistent administration of the tests were refined, and more countries participated in the testing. Whether it was due to changes in the tests or improvement in students' learning, American students did score somewhat better. Out of thirty-five countries participating in the IEA's 2007 Trends in International Mathematics and Science Study (TIMSS) fourth-grade tests, American students ranked 11th in math and 8th in science. On the eighth-grade tests, the U.S. ranked 9th in math and 11th in science

Table 8.1

First International Mathematics and Science Achievement Test Scores (mid-1960s)

	Participating educational systems	US rank
Mathematics		
Age 13	12	11
High school seniors:		
math students	12	12
non-math	10	10
Science		
Age 10	12	4
Age 14	14	7
High school seniors	14	14

Source: Medrich and Griffith, 1992

out of the 45 countries participating.[3] Some of the relative improvement in the U.S. ranking, however, had to do with the large number of low-scoring developing countries included in the TIMSS studies.

The Organisation for Economic Co-operation and Development (OECD) has sponsored a second international testing regimen, the *Programme for International Student Assessment* (PISA), conducted on three-year intervals since 2000, with fifty-seven countries participating in the 2006 study. The PISA tests have several advantages over the TIMSS. PISA includes tests in reading and problem solving in addition to math and science. The tests are said to emphasize "important knowledge and skills needed in adult life." Students are targeted by age (fifteen-year-olds) rather than grade level, and the PISA offers a more consistent comparison group when the analysis is limited to just the thirty (or more) OECD member countries.[4]

Again, the United States fared poorly. Five OECD countries scored lower than the United States on the 2009 mathematics test: Spain, Italy, Greece, Turkey, and Mexico (figure 8.1).[5]

When the *Nation at Risk* report was written in 1983, the American higher education system was the envy of the world. In the United States today, the oldest working-age cohort (the cohort that was the youngest in 1983) is more likely to be college educated than the same cohort in any other nation (figure 8.2). In most other countries, however, each new generation is more educated than the one preceding it. In his 2011 State of the Union address, President Obama remarked, "America has fallen to ninth [actually

Figure 8.1. Performance of 15-year-olds in Science, Reading, and Mathematics (PISA), U.S. (line) and 29 OECD Nations (boxplots), 2000–2009.

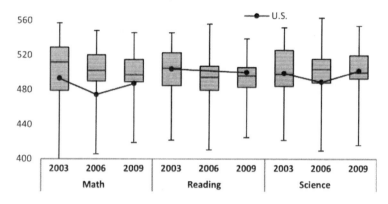

Source: OECD, Society at a Glance, 2009

Figure 8.2. High School and College Degree Attainment, by Age, U.S. (line) and 28 OECD Nations (boxplots), 2006.

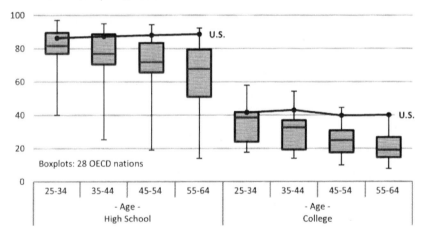

Source: OECD, Education at a Glance, 2010.

tenth] in the proportion of young people with a college degree. . . . By the end of the decade, America will once again have the highest proportion of college graduates in the world." In the case of high school graduation rates, the United States also has an elderly workforce better educated than the younger generation.

The United States is also well behind most other countries in awarding degrees in math, science, and engineering. On average, OECD nations award over 22 percent of their bachelor's degrees in math, science, and engineering fields. The United States ranks 23rd, with just over 16 percent of its degrees in these fields.[6]

The failure of the United States to keep pace in college graduation is partly accounted for by the high cost of American higher education. In terms of both the overall spending and the cost per student in tuition and fees, the United States substantially exceeds any other nation. The United States spends 3.1 percent of its GDP on higher education, twice the average for OECD nations (Canada is second at 2.6 percent). In addition, other countries' public university tuition and fees are a small fraction of what American universities charge, and many countries do not charge students at all to attend public universities, or are just beginning to charge.

Reliability of International Education Measures

Many factors affect the reliability of the cross-national measures of educational achievement. The exams have to be translated into each country's native language, and the comparability of test items, especially those involving more than simple mathematical expressions, may be affected by differences in language and vocabulary. The American students scored slightly above average on the 2009 PISA reading test, but designing comparable reading tests in different languages is an uncertain science. In math and science, differences in curriculum (at a given grade level some students may be studying geometry in one country, algebra in another) or the time of the school year when the tests are administered may also affect results.

Most problematic are situations where positive features of the school system lead to misleadingly negative test score results. The United States has been a leader among the world's nations in mainstreaming students with learning disabilities in regular classrooms. In other countries, many students with disabilities are more often schooled separately and may or may not be included in the national testing. When the First International Science Study tests were administered to high school seniors in 1969, the United States led the world in terms of the percentage of the senior-year age cohort that was still enrolled in school, in part because many states required attendance up to age eighteen. Other countries either had higher dropout rates or, as in the case of West Germany, tracked working-class students into technical and vocational schools where the tests were not administered. As seen in figure 8.3, the exceptionally high rates of school enrollment in the United States accounted for the poor performance of high school seniors on the science test.

A good understanding of who is and who is not being tested is crucial to any analysis of educational statistics. In the case of most international

Figure 8.3. Enrollment and First International Science Study Results: Last Year of Secondary School.

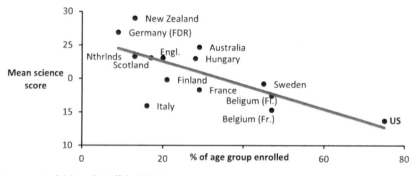

Source: Medrich and Griffith (1992).

tests, the sampling begins with nationwide random samples of schools, and the tests are given either to all students or to a sample of students in attendance in the selected schools. In the case of the PISA tests, the sample includes those schools that customarily enroll fifteen-year-olds (perhaps excluding American fifteen-year-olds held back in eighth grade) and then a sample of fifteen-year-olds within those schools.

Unlike the educational systems of almost every other country in the world, which are run by centralized national or provincial education bureaucracies, American education is highly localized. Some argue that this accounts for the relatively poor performance of American students on international tests, as the United States has lagged in the development of national curricular standards and tests to measure student performance. Local control has meant that the administration of international tests in the United States often depends on the voluntary participation of local school authorities. In other countries, a single national education bureaucracy can require that schools administer the international tests and assure uniform administration of those tests; in the United States, this requires the consent of local school boards or school principals. As a result, the United States typically has the lowest rates of participation in the tests. In the First International Science Study, only 43 percent of the sampled American schools agreed to participate, while Australia, Hungary, Finland, and New Zealand had participation rates exceeding 98 percent.[7] In the 2003 PISA study, 82 of the 220 U.S. schools sampled refused to participate.[8] In the 2007 eighth-grade TIMSS tests, of the 42 countries participating, only Hong Kong had a lower school participation rate than the United States.[9]

One should always be suspicious of self-selection bias due to low response rates on education test scores. If the choice of participating in a study is given to school principals, one should expect that the principals who are most confident of their students' abilities may be most likely to agree to participate. Alternatively, participation may be highest in school districts where the school district bureaucracy exercises the most authority over the school principals. Low student response rates should also be suspected of contributing to artificially high test scores. The best students are least likely to be absent on the day the tests are given. When the tests are used to evaluate the performance of teachers and administrators, there may be ways of assuring that the weakest students are more likely to be absent, suspended, or in detention on test days.

Analyzing International Education Data

In addition to being used for cross-national comparisons of education system performance, the international tests are used in research assessing the relationships between student achievement and cross-national and within-nation differences in school resources, curricula, approaches to teaching, family background, and home environment. For this purpose, the international studies also collect data on student demographics, school curriculum, school resources, and student attitudes toward schooling. One discovery of the early mathematics studies was that other countries were successfully teaching advanced mathematical concepts at an earlier age than American educators thought possible.[10]

A general finding of much of the research on educational achievement is that school resources, measured by factors such as the amount of money spent per pupil, teacher salaries, and class size, have little effect on what students learn. As shown in the case of the PISA tests (figure 8.4), there is a weak positive correlation between school spending and achievement, and lack of money certainly does not account for the poor U.S. test performance. A surprising finding of the first and second IEA Mathematics and Science studies was that the countries with the largest class sizes (often, Asian countries) had the highest achievement scores. On the latest PISA test, there was a strong correlation between class size (or, the student-teacher ratio) and educational achievement, but it is the opposite of what one might expect: Countries with higher student-teacher ratios tend to have higher scores (figure 8.5).

The same studies that show that school resources have little effect on educational achievement also report that family resources have a strong influence. The consistent finding of educational research that students' family background, measured by the parents' occupational status, income, wealth, and level of education are the strongest determinants of educational

Figure 8.4. PISA Math, Science, and Reading Scores and School Spending, % of GDP.

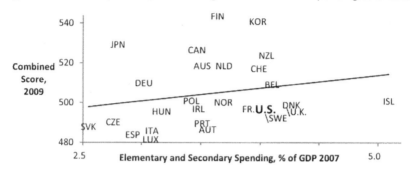

Source: OECD, 2009 PISA Results; OECD, Education at a Glance, 2010.

Figure 8.5. PISA Math, Science, and Reading Scores and Students per Teacher.

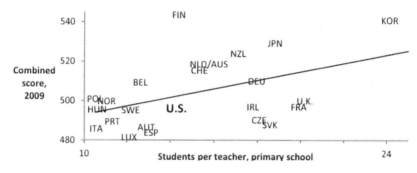

Source: OECD, 2009 PISA Results; OECD Education at a Glance, 2010.

achievement represents a critical constraint on all the world's education systems. In all countries, there is a large gap in the scores of children from one-parent and two-parent families (figure 8.6), but the size of the gap is greatest in the United States.

The Validity of Standardized Tests

For the most part, standardized educational tests measure a mixture of aptitude and achievement. Aptitude tests are designed to measure intellectual ability separate from what students learn in the classroom. IQ tests are the purest form of an aptitude test: No matter what you have learned from your teachers, your IQ score changes very little from first grade to your senior year of college. The more closely a standardized test measures the mastery of a specific curriculum and subject matter, the more it measures achievement.

Figure 8.6. PISA Reading and Math, by Family Status, 2009: U.S. (line) and 33 OECD Nations (boxplots).

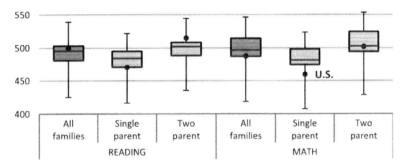

Source: NCES, International Data Explorer.

The history of the SAT illustrates the subtle distinction between an aptitude test and an achievement test. When the test was first created in 1901, "SAT" stood for "Scholastic Achievement Test," but in 1941, the name was changed to "Scholastic Aptitude Test." In 1990, the SAT was renamed "Scholastic Assessment Test," with no clear indication of just what the test was assessing. Each of these changes reflected the intellectual fads and education politics of the time rather than any changes in what the test actually did measure. Matters were settled once and for all in 1994 when the name was changed to just plain SAT. This was three years after Kentucky Fried Chicken became KFC, for much the same reason.

So what does the SAT measure, and is it a valid measure of whatever it measures? There has been extensive debate and research concerning the validity of the SAT as a measure of individual academic achievement and ability.[11] Are the tests culturally biased? Does instruction in test-taking skills improve students' scores? Are there other kinds of intelligence that the test does not measure? How well does the test predict students' academic success in college?

Regardless of whether the SAT is a valid measure of individual intelligence or learning, its validity as an aggregate social indicator depends on how it is used. The average SAT score of a freshman class is a very good measure of how stringent a college's admissions standards are, and increasing freshman SAT scores are a reasonable indicator that a college is becoming more competitive. For a long time, trends in SAT scores, particularly the declining scores of the 1970s and 1980s, were cited as a general indicator of the quality of the nation's elementary and secondary education. For the most part, such conclusions were not valid, as changes in the percentage of high school students taking the test were the primary reason for the decline.

Whether improvement in group SAT scores indicates educational improvements, as was suggested by the Simpson's paradox example in chapter 3 (table 3.2), depends on whether you think the changing racial composition of test-takers is a valid excuse for the stagnating total scores.

TESTING AMERICAN STUDENTS

On July 1, 1966, the U.S. Office of Education released what came to be known as the *Coleman Report*, a national study of educational achievement, conducted by sociologist James S. Coleman, based on verbal and mathematics tests administered to 600,000 students and 60,000 teachers in 4,000 schools.[12] Coleman's findings were so surprising, and disappointing to those who favored increases in federal education spending, that the Office of Education chose the day before the Fourth of July weekend to release the results in hopes that newspapers would not pay too much attention.[13] The findings, carefully hidden in the summaries of the report distributed at the press conference and buried in the back of the full report, were that school resources (school spending, class size, teachers' salaries, and school facilities) had little effect on student achievement and that the socioeconomic status of the students' families was the primary determinant of how well students did in school. Subsequent research has largely confirmed the main findings, and the report was significant in that it led to new efforts to measure what American students were learning and to significant advances in the statistical analysis of standardized education test score data.

The Nation's Report Card

Since 1969, more systematic national testing of student learning has been conducted under the auspices of the *National Assessment of Education Progress* (NAEP), sometimes called the Nation's Report Card. The NAEP regularly tests a national sample of about 7,000 students in grades four, eight, and twelve (or ages nine, thirteen, and seventeen) in mathematics, science, reading, and writing, and in other subjects on an intermittent basis. In addition to the subject matter testing, the NAEP also collects data on school and classroom characteristics, student demographics, and student home environments. The NAEP sample is too small to provide scores for individual schools, and only limited data for large cities and the fifty states are available, but it provides the best data for assessing national trends in student achievement and for evaluating general relationships between student achievement and other factors.

TABLE 8.2
NAEP Reading and Math Scores, 1971-08

				Net Change	
Reading	1971	1999	2008	'71-08	'99-08
age 9	208	212	220	+12	+8
age 13	255	259	260	+4	+0
age 17	285	288	286	+1	-2
Math	1978	1999	2008	'78-08	'99-08
age 9	219	232	243	+24	+11
age 13	264	276	281	+17	+5
age 17	300	308	306	+6	-2

Source: NAEP Data Explorer, Long-term trends

NAEP tests are scaled with a mean of about 150 at each grade level, but for the math, reading, and science tests, the NAEP rescales the tests on a common "scale score," with a theoretical maximum score of 500, to allow for comparisons between different grade levels. Over time, there has been some improvement in student scale scores on the NAEP tests, particularly in elementary school math (table 8.2; see also figure 6.2).

The Racial Gap in Educational Achievement

The persistent racial and ethnic learning disparities are the most troubling finding of the American educational research. As noted in chapter 2, African American and Latino students are graduating from high school with an eighth-grade level of education. Using the math scale-score data, seventeen-year-old black and Hispanic students score about the same as thirteen-year-old whites (table 8.3). On the positive side, there has been some narrowing of the black–white gap.

Note that at ages nine and thirteen, the improvements for all students are less than the improvements for each racial and ethnic group. This is an example of Simpson's paradox and is due to the declining proportion of whites among the students tested.

The gaps narrow but do not disappear when one controls for measures of the students' family background. In the case of the NAEP science scores, shown in figure 8.7, the gap between Hispanic and white students' scores is reduced when comparing children of mothers with the same level of education, but the black–white gap narrows less.

TABLE 8.3
NAEP Math by Age, Race and Ethnicity

	1978	1999	2008	Net Change	
				78-08	'99-08
Age 9					
White	224	239	250	+26	+11
Black	192	211	224	+32	+13
Hispanic	203	213	234	+31	+21
Other	227	243	256	+29	+13
All students	219	232	243	+24	+11
Age 13					
White	272	283	290	+18	+7
Black	230	251	262	+32	+11
Hispanic	238	259	268	+30	+8
Other	273	283	296	+23	+13
All students	264	276	281	+17	+5
Age 17					
White	306	315	314	+8	-1
Black	268	283	287	+19	+4
Hispanic	276	293	293	+16	0
Other	313	320	316	+3	-3
All students	300	308	306	+6	-2

Source: NAEP Data Explorer, Long-term trends

In reading, there has been some improvement in the black–white learning gap in the elementary schools, but the scores for black high school students have not improved since the mid-1980s. The lack of improvement at the high school level, however, may be due to a substantial decline in the black high school dropout rate over this time.

The literature on the racial learning gap points to three possible explanations. Some authors, such as Jonathan Kozol, place the blame on racial disparities in school funding and racial segregation.[14] The United States has the most unequal system of school finance in the developed world, and the racial segregation in many of the nation's school systems surpasses the level of segregation at the time of the 1954 *Brown v. Board of Education* decision. More conservative scholars, such as Abigail Thernstrom and Stephan Thernstrom, point to culture and the home environment.[15] The racial disparities in learning, they argue, correlate strongly with racial differences in the prevalence of single-parent families, television viewing, and parental

Figure 8.7. NAEP Reading Scores, by Race and Mother's Education, 2008.

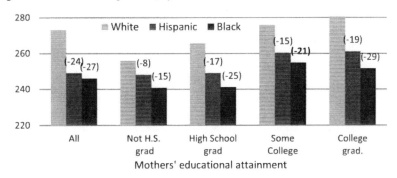

Source: NAEP Data Explorer.

academic expectations. Still a third perspective, represented by Richard Rothstein, argues that the racial and ethnic disparities merely mask the socioeconomic disparities in income, wealth, and parental education.[16] To eliminate the gap in educational achievement, he argues, we should first do something about the gaps in income and wealth.

Each of these perspectives is deeply involved in the controversy over a multitude of policy solutions designed to address the problem: school finance reform, bilingual education, multicultural education, school busing, preschool education, school vouchers, charter schools, smaller class size, smaller schools, longer school days, longer school years, same-sex schools, social promotion, training in parenting skills, and different approaches to school discipline and the teaching of reading and mathematics.

No Child Left Behind Testing

Under the No Child Left Behind (NCLB) law, signed by President George W. Bush on January 8, 2002, educational measurement reached its zenith in the United States, at least in terms of the amount, if not the quality, of testing. While the NAEP surveys a sample of only 7,000 students per subject at three grade levels, NCLB tests all students in grades three through eight and eleven in mathematics and reading. Science tests are administered to all students at three grade levels. Where the NAEP samples are too small to provide reliable data for individual schools and school districts, the explicit purpose of NCLB testing is to measure the schools' performance. Unlike the NAEP, the NCLB data have no sampling error, but interpreting the test results is fraught with reliability and validity pitfalls.

Under NCLB, each state is required to set "adequate yearly progress" (AYP) standards for its schools based on the percentage of students whose test scores meet a state-defined level of proficiency. The proficiency standard applies not only to the entire student body but to each of several groups of students defined by race, ethnicity, low income ("school lunch eligible"), limited English proficiency, and learning disability (students with "individualized education plans").

Schools that fail to make AYP in one year (for any of the subgroups) and those that fail to improve in the second year are classified as "in need of improvement." The schools in need of improvement do not, as is often claimed, have their funding reduced; they actually become eligible for additional federal funds, and students in the need-improvement schools may be given the opportunity to change schools or receive tutorial assistance. Only if the schools fail for several years are they expected to implement more stringent policy changes, including reassigning or firing staff. In theory, the percentage of students who must be proficient to meet the AYP goals will increase each year until 2014, when all students will be expected to be proficient. This, and the fact that students classified as learning disabled or with limited English proficiency are expected to meet the same proficiency standard as other students, are among the more problematic aspects of the law.

Reliability and Validity of No Child Left Behind Data

Because the states design their own NCLB exams and set their own standards for what constitutes "proficiency," national AYP test results and cross-state comparisons of the test results, including the percentage of students who are proficient or the percentage of schools that meet AYP, are essentially meaningless. This is best demonstrated in a comparison of the percentage of students who meet state proficiency standards and the states' average scores on the NAEP exam. Only 2 states, Massachusetts and Minnesota, have over half of their eighth-grade students meeting the national NAEP math proficiency standards (to achieve this requires approximately a 290 average score). Nevertheless, in 36 states, not including Massachusetts, over half of the students meet their states' proficiency standard. State pass rates only weakly correlate with the national standards (figure 8.8).

Within states, comparisons of year-to-year changes in NCLB test scores and AYP rates also pose problems of measurement reliability. Whereas the NAEP carefully maintains consistent measurement standards for the time series trend data it reports, state NCLB tests and standards often change. Because governors and state boards of education can be held publicly accountable for both the percentage of students who meet standards and the number of schools that make adequate progress, they have an incentive to make changes that make them look good. This can involve making

Figure 8.8. State NCLB Standards and NAEP Scores, 8th-Grade Math, 2005.

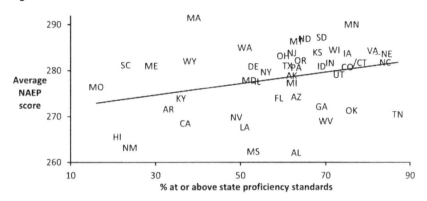

Sources: Education Week, Education Counts Research Center; NAEP Data Explorer

improvements in the tests in ways that happen to improve scores, such as adjusting the weighting of components of the tests, changing the policies on the special accommodations offered students with learning disabilities, or raising the minimum number of students needed for schools' subgroup population scores to be counted (the minimum subgroup size varies from fifteen to two hundred across the states).

Even in those states that do maintain a consistent testing regimen, several factors inherent in the testing threaten the validity of many conclusions drawn from trends in NCLB results. By 2007, eighth-grade students had taken NCLB tests in each of their previous five years of schooling, and some improvement in their scores would be expected due to a "testing effect": students learn how to take the exams more efficiently. On the other hand, there may be a reverse testing effect at work. Students may become less motivated to do well on the tests as they learn that their scores on the tests do not affect their grades.

Improvements in scores may also reflect a "teaching to the test" phenomenon. As schools and teachers become more aware of the kinds of questions asked and the subject matter that is emphasized in the test, they may change what they emphasize in their teaching. To some extent, this is a good thing, as teachers adjust their teaching to state curricular standards. A similar problem may occur as schools and school districts focus their resources on the subjects that are tested and place less emphasis on subjects that are not tested, such as art, music, physical education, and history.

Nevertheless, if the NCLB tests are well designed, they do provide reliable and generally valid measures of differences in student achievement in the subjects tested across schools and school districts in the same state. This is to say that, on average, students in schools that score well on the math, reading, and science tests are indeed better at math, reading, and science than students in schools that score poorly. But this does not mean that the schools' test scores are good measures of the quality of the education that the schools provide. American public schools tend to be highly segregated by race, ethnicity, and wealth, and these and related attributes of students' family background have much more to do with differences in school scores than what goes on in the classroom. To evaluate the quality of the education schools provide, these factors have to be taken into account.

THE WORST SCHOOLS IN THE NATION?

In 1987, U.S. Secretary of Education William Bennett announced that the Chicago public schools were the "worst in the nation." Bennett's evidence was based on high school students' scores on the American College Test (ACT). Half of Chicago's high schools scored in the bottom 1 percent of the schools that took the test.[17] Until the No Child Left Behind law was enacted, there were no better measures of the overall quality of most of the nation's school districts than scores on ACT and SAT tests. And these were pretty poor indicators. Only students hoping to attend four-year colleges took the tests. Schools that encouraged more students to take the tests typically saw their average scores go down. Because only 6 percent of Illinois high school students take the SAT, the state often scores near the top of the state rankings.

Nevertheless, a cursory examination of the NCLB data suggests that Chicago schools are not doing well. Chicago public school students consistently do worse on the state tests, in each subject and at every grade level, than students in the state of Illinois as a whole. In 2010, just 70 percent of Chicago elementary school students passed the state's NCLB tests, called the Illinois Standards Achievement Test (ISAT), compared to 81 percent statewide (including Chicago; the Illinois pass rate excluding Chicago would have been about 86 percent).

However, Chicago schools serve a student body that is substantially different from that of the rest of the state: 87 percent of Chicago public school students qualify for the school lunch program, compared to only 45 percent statewide, and over 87 percent of Chicago students are black or Hispanic, compared to less than 40 percent statewide. In 2010, 370 Chicago public elementary schools, over 75 percent of the district's schools, had combined pass rates on all tests below the state's 77.5 percent AYP goal. In addition, the schools must meet attendance standards and pass-rate standard for each test and each demographic group. In every school that failed to achieve the standard, more than half the students were classified as low income, as

Figure 8.9. Percentage of Students Meeting or Exceeding 2010 NCLB Standards and % Student Body Low-Income, 479 Chicago Elementary Schools (all tests).

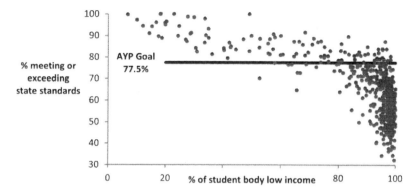

Source: Illinois Report Card data file.

determined by their eligibility for the school lunch program (see figure 8.9). In 2012, unless Congress changes the law, the pass-rate standard will be 92.5 percent. Only 17 out of 479 Chicago schools met that standard in 2010.

Closing the Gap?

Nevertheless, the release of the 2006 ISAT scores was greeted with cheers. The *Chicago Tribune* announced the results in March 2007 with the head-line: "Chicago Schools See Huge Gains on Test Score." The story reported that Chicago students' 62 percent pass rate on all the elementary grade tests was substantially higher than the 48 percent pass rate for 2005. The results were "extraordinarily encouraging," according to Chicago Public School system CEO Arne Duncan, and district officials credited the gains to policy changes, including "after-school tutoring, better-trained teachers and new classroom assessments."[18] Duncan is presently the U.S. Secretary of Education.

The *Tribune* story did note that some might attribute the improvement to changes made to the tests.[19] The 2006 ISAT offered students more time to complete tests with fewer questions, an improved answer sheet, and color illustrations. The state lowered the passing score for the eighth-grade math test to make it more in line with the scores in the lower grades. Subsequent stories reported other test changes that may have affected the results, such as giving less weight to the relatively difficult "response" items and more to multiple-choice questions.[20] There were good reasons for most of these changes, and they may have resulted in more valid tests, but the changes undermined the reliability of year-to-year comparisons.

In a letter to the *Tribune,* Rufus Williams, president of the Chicago Board of Education, responded to critics who suggested that the changes in the test were the reason Chicago's students did so well:

> Our children can learn. They can achieve and they can compete. Their performance on the 2006 ISAT is but one measure of proof. To continually question their record-breaking results demonstrates an inability to believe that they can actually meet the high expectations that we must set for them. They are proving they can.[21]

This is an interesting counterargument, equivalent to the Bush administration claims that those who criticized his management of the Iraq War were actually criticizing the performance of the troops in the field. The next step in the argument is to claim that those who question the success of the administration's efforts are actually encouraging its failure. But Williams cited hard evidence to support his claim: The Chicago students' gains were substantially higher than those of the students in the rest of Illinois:

> Officials across the state agree that districts made gains all over Illinois, but Chicago Public Schools students led the way, gaining 14 percentage points on the test, compared to the overall state gain of 8 percentage points.[22]

Williams makes what might be a valid point: Changes in the test may account for the statewide increase, but that doesn't explain why Chicago's improvement was better than the rest of the state's. Unfortunately, Williams's analysis involves a closing-the-gap fallacy, involving comparisons of changes starting from different base numbers. It is true that the Chicago scores did improve from a 48 percent pass rate to 62 percent, while the Illinois scores improved from 69 percent to 77 percent (table 8.4). But look what happens if we recalculate the test results to show the percentage of students who failed. Chicago's failure rate went down 27 percent; Illinois' failure rate went down 26 percent. There is no meaningful difference between the two results (indeed, the 1 point difference may be due to the rounding of the base scores).

Evidence That Chicago Schools Are Doing Well

So far the data suggest that Chicago students are less proficient than students in the rest of the state and that there is no reliable evidence that student performance improved either in Chicago or statewide in 2006. Nevertheless, a closer look at the city and state data offers some evidence that

TABLE 8.4

Chicago and Illinois ISAT Results, 2005-6

	2005	2006	Net Change	% Change
Passing rate				
Chicago Public Schools	48%	62%	+14	+29%
All Illinois Public Schools	69	77	+8	+12
Failure rate				
Chicago Public Schools	52	38	-14	-27
All Illinois Public Schools	31	23	-8	-26

Source: Illinois State Board of Education, 2005-6 Report Card

the Chicago public school system may be doing a better job of educating students than the school systems in the rest of the state.

The data in figure 8.10 tell the story. Let's begin with the reading pass rate for "all students" enrolled in the third grade. On the 2010 ISAT tests, 76 percent of Chicago students passed the third-grade math test compared to 86 percent for the state as a whole, a 10 percentage point difference.[23] But almost all of the state–city gap disappears when we look at the subgroup scores. Over half of the third-grade city–state gap is explained by the greater proportion of black, Hispanic, and low-income students in the Chicago schools.

The strongest evidence in defense of the Chicago schools is seen when we examine the eighth-grade math results, where the city–state gap for all students is 7 percentage points.[24] More telling, however, is that Hispanic,

Figure 8.10. Gap between Illinois and Chicago 3rd- and 8th-Grade Math Pass Rates, 2010 (positive difference = Illinois higher).

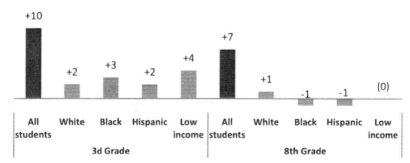

Source: Illinois Interactive Report Card.

black, and low-income eighth-grade students do just as well or better in Chicago as they do in Illinois as a whole, and whites do nearly as well.

It is difficult to imagine how anything other than better teaching in the Chicago schools might account for these results, but there are some alternative explanations. It is unlikely that there are any major differences in the family background of third-grade and eighth-grade students in either Chicago or the rest of the state. There might be something peculiar about the eighth-grade test, but other research shows the relative improvements in Chicago scores occur gradually over five grade levels from third to eighth.[25] One possible factor might be attendance. Chicago schools at all grade levels do have a slightly lower attendance rate than schools statewide; it is likely that eighth-grade attendance is worse than third-grade attendance, but no data support or disprove this. Differences in school policies regarding social promotion—promoting students to the next grade regardless of their proficiency in the grade-level subject matter—might explain the results. Chicago eliminated social promotion in 1996 and now requires that students pass a third-, sixth-, and eighth-grade exam to be promoted to the next grade. Holding students back in grade results in older students at each grade level (a positive effect on test scores) especially in the upper grade levels, but it also results in weaker students taking the test twice (and this may have a negative effect). Unfortunately, there are no clear data for the rest of the Illinois school districts to examine the effect.

Searching for Excuses

Until the No Child Left Behind law was passed, there was very little systematic measurement of what students were actually learning in many of our nation's schools; but even with the law, cherry picking and misleading interpretations of NCLB test results are commonplace. There is an understandable tendency for school officials to tout the initial aggregate results if they are positive, to look at other comparisons if they are not, and if those comparisons are not good, to search for other explanations that offer a positive spin on what is going on in the schools. Often this is more than justified, but the process is one-sided and leaves out the search for evidence that might explain away the positive results. This is unfortunate, because the law works best when school officials uncover disappointing results and make meaningful changes to address the problems.

When the 2006 eleventh-grade Illinois high school test scores, released a week after the elementary tests, showed a slight decline in both the Illinois

Figure 8.11. Illinois 11th-Grade Students: % Meeting or Exceeding State Standards.

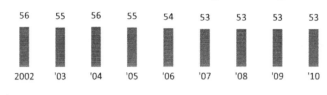

Source: Illinois Interactive Report Card.

and Chicago ISAT results, state officials had an explanation: The eleventh graders did not have the benefit of the regular testing that had so dramatically improved the elementary students' performance. "Our kids in 11th grade didn't start their careers in standards-based classrooms," explained state assessment director Becky McCabe. "Those 17-year-olds haven't had the same kind of instruction our elementary kids are getting now."[26] Maybe. But maybe it was because there were no changes in the eleventh-grade exam, which was designed by a different company.

McCabe's explanation for the high school decline and the elementary school increase is that the elementary school students had been exposed to up to five years of ISAT standards (the first elementary exams were administered in 2002), while the 17-year-olds had only two years' experience under the new standards (in 2002 and 2003 when they were in seventh and eighth grade). Unfortunately, four years later, with eleventh graders who did start their careers in "standards-based classrooms" as third graders in 2002, there had been no net improvement (figure 8.11).

Essentially, the assessment director found reasons to dismiss the disappointing high school results, to embrace the seemingly positive elementary results, and to wait until the things that improved the elementary school scores begin to affect the high schools. No doubt, this will happen when the state discovers a reason for including more color graphics or lowering the passing grade on the high school tests.

If Chicago's schools have improved since the education secretary called them the "worst in the nation," it is because they took seriously the test score results on which the secretary based his conclusion. The district instituted far-reaching reforms, including decentralizing the school district bureaucracy, holding principals accountable to elected school councils, and eliminating social promotion. None of this would have happened if they had found a way to explain away the results.

NOTES

1. National Commission on Excellence in Education, *A Nation at Risk: The Imperative for Educational Reform*, April 1983, at http://www.ed.gov/pubs/NatAtRisk/index .html.

2. National Commission on Excellence in Education, *A Nation at Risk*.

3. Patrick Gonzales, *Highlights from TIMSS 2007: Mathematics and Science Achievement of U.S. Fourth- and Eighth-Grade Students in an International Context* (NCES 2009–001Revised) (Washington, DC: National Center for Education Statistics, Institute of Education Sciences, U.S. Department of Education, September 2009), table A-1.

4. Organisation for Economic Co-operation and Development, "OECD Programme for International Student Assessment," at http://www.pisa.oecd.org.

5. The scores for the 2006 U.S. reading tests were invalidated because someone forgot to proofread the exam booklets.

6. OECD, *Education at a Glance 2010: OECD Indicators*, September 10, 2010, table B.3.07, at http://www.oecd-ilibrary.org/education/education-at-a-glance -2010_eag-2010-en.

7. Elliott A. Medrich and Jeanne Griffith, *International Mathematics and Science Assessment: What Have We Learned?* Report no. CNES 92-011 (Washington, DC: U.S. Department of Education, Office of Educational Research and Improvement, 1992), at http://nces.ed.gov/pubs92/92011.pdf.

8. Elart von Collan, "OECD PISA—An Example of Stochastic Illiteracy?" *Economic Quality Control* 16, no. 2 (2001): 227–53, at www.heldermann-verlag.de/eqc/eqc01_16/ eqc16016.pdf.

9. Gonzales, *Highlights from TIMSS 2007*, table A-1.

10. Medrich and Griffith, *International Mathematics and Science Assessment*, 35.

11. Nicholas Lemann, *The Big Test: The Secret History of the American Meritocracy* (New York: Farrar, Straus & Giroux, 1999).

12. James S. Coleman, Ernest Q. Campbell, Carol J. Hobson, et al., *Equality of Educational Opportunity* (Washington, DC: U.S. Government Printing Office, 1966).

13. Gerald Grant, "Shaping Social Policy: The Politics of the Coleman Report," *Teachers College Record* 75, no. 1 (September 1973): 17–54.

14. Jonathan Kozol, *The Shame of the Nation: The Restoration of Apartheid Schooling in America* (New York: Crown, 2005).

15. Stephan Thernstrom and Abigail Thernstrom, *No Excuses: Closing the Racial Gap in Learning* (New York: Simon & Schuster, 2003).

16. Richard Rothstein, *Class and Schools: Using Social, Economic and Educational Reform to Close the Black–White Achievement Gap* (Washington, DC: Economic Policy Institute, 2004).

17. "Schools in Chicago Are Called the Worst by Education Chief," *New York Times*, November 8, 1987, at http://www.nytimes.com/1987/11/08/us/schools-in-chicago-are -called-the-worst-by-education-chief.html.

18. Tracy Dell'Angela, "Chicago Schools See Huge Gains on Test Scores," *Chicago Tribune*, March 6, 2007, 1.

19. In 2004, a new contractor, Harcourt Assessment, was chosen to redesign the tests. This, just after Harcourt hired a former aide and political adviser to the governor as a lobbyist. See Naarah Patton, "Harcourt Contract: Saga of a Fiasco," April 11, 2006, at http://www.susanohanian.org/atrocity_fetch.php?id=5862.

20. Diane Rado, "Scoring Method on ISAT Faulted: Big Gains Could Have Been Inflated, State Adviser Says," *Chicago Tribune*, April 13, 2007, 1.

21. Rufus Williams, "Students' Performance Has Amazed All," *Chicago Tribune*, March 21, 2007, Letters to the Editor.

22. Williams, "Students' Performance Has Amazed All."

23. Note that the Chicago scores are included in the Illinois scores; the gap between Chicago and the rest of the state is greater, over 13 percentage points.

24. One should not make too much of "all students" change from third to eighth grade, as these are different tests and the smaller gap may be due to less variation in the eighth-grade scores.

25. John Q. Easton, Stuart Luppescu, and Todd Rosenkranz, "2006 ISAT Reading and Math Scores in Chicago and the Rest of the State," Consortium on Chicago School Research at the University of Chicago, June 2007, at ccsr.uchicago.edu/content/publications.php?pub_id=115.

26. Rosalind Rossi, Art Golab, and Kate N. Grossman, "Tardy State High School Scores Show Few Gains: Science, Reading Down, but Math Results Up a Bit," *Chicago Sun-Times*, March 13, 2007, 16.

Measuring Poverty and Inequality

> You are entitled to your own opinion, but you're not entitled to your own facts.
>
> —DANIEL PATRICK MOYNIHAN

DO FREE markets and globalization foster greater or lesser poverty and inequality in the developing world? Does international development assistance to third world nations alleviate or exacerbate the conditions of poverty? Do welfare state social policies significantly reduce poverty in developed nations? What impact did the U.S. 1996 welfare reform act have on the nation's poor? Are the relatively high rates of poverty in the United States due to the dysfunctional behavior of the poor, to racism and discrimination, or to stingy social policies? How do these factors account for the feminization of poverty in the United States? Is it true that "the rich are getting richer and the poor, poorer"?

The arguments, policy evaluations, political debates, and academic research concerning these questions rely on measurements of the incidence of poverty. Poverty rates generally measure the percentage of the population living in households whose annual income (or, as we shall see, annual consumption) falls below a predetermined poverty threshold. There are two different approaches to defining what level of standard of living constitutes poverty. Absolute poverty thresholds define a level below which households lack basic necessary goods and services. Relative thresholds measure the percentage of the population living at a standard well below the average of their fellow citizens.

Neither strategy for defining poverty is ideal. Poverty is relative, and absolute standards of measuring it are inherently arbitrary. Relative poverty thresholds measure inequality more than they measure a consistent level of deprivation. For these and other reasons, debates about poverty often end up being debates about the measurement of poverty. Liberal scholars[1] often argue that poverty rate statistics underestimate the true dimensions of poverty and that higher poverty thresholds should be used, while conservatives[2] insist that the statistics exaggerate poverty, either because the thresholds are set too low or because the measure of family income does not include all the resources available to the families who are classified as poor.

MEASURING POVERTY IN DEVELOPING NATIONS

Since the early 1980s, two indicators developed by the World Bank have been the standard measures of poverty in low- and middle-income nations. The bank defines "extreme poverty" as the percentage of a country's population living in households consuming less than $1.25 a day (sometimes referred to as $1 a day), in 2005 dollars. For wealthier or middle-income countries, such as most South American nations, a $2 a day threshold is used as the more general poverty indicator.[3] Both thresholds are expressed in constant U.S. dollars and are adjusted for price differences in consumer goods between countries, using measures of national currencies' purchasing power parity (PPP). In a country with an average family size of four persons, the $1.25 a day standard would mean a family poverty threshold of $1,825 per year. In some countries, the poverty measures are based on the number of persons in families with incomes below the poverty threshold, but in the poorest nations (where subsistence agriculture and noncash economies predominate), the indicators use estimates of consumption—the value of the goods and services consumed by families.

The World Bank estimates that a total of 1.4 billion people lived in extreme poverty in 2005, a reduction from almost 1.8 billion in 1990 and 1.9 billion in 1981. Twenty-seven percent of the developing world's population lived in extreme poverty in 2005, half the 1981 rate.

Over the past three decades, regional trends in the international poverty rate (figure 9.1) indicate that the poverty rate has declined dramatically in most of Asia, has remained high in Africa and in the countries of the former Soviet Union, and has held relatively constant throughout the Middle East and Latin America. The most dramatic reductions in poverty have been in India and China. In China alone, 625 million fewer people lived in poverty in 2005 than in 1981. Excluding China, the rest of the world has seen a net increase in the number of persons living in extreme poverty. Although the poverty rate for sub-Saharan Africa has decreased slightly, the number of poor persons in that region nearly doubled, from 212 million to 388 million.[4]

Figure 9.1. Regional Extreme Poverty Rates, 1981–2005 (% below $1.25 a day, 2005 $).

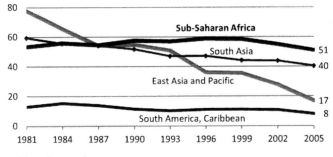

Source: World Bank, PovcalNet

Poverty is just one of several indicators reported in the World Bank's annual *World Development Report,* a widely respected source of statistical information on trends in poverty and related social conditions.[5] In the report and on its website, the bank presents detailed information on national accounts (e.g., GDP, national income, and trade data), business conditions, governmental policies, and developmental assistance. The United Nations provides similar data on its website and in a series of annual and regional *Human Development Reports.*[6] Although much of the data is the same, the tone of the two reports reflects the ideologies of the countries in control of the organizations. The World Bank tends to see poverty as something to be addressed by economic development; the United Nations stresses that alleviating poverty and inequality will have the side benefit of promoting economic development.

In 2000, the United Nations adopted the Millennium Declaration, setting eight broad development goals for developing nations relating to various aspects of poverty, education, gender inequality, health, and environment (table 9.1). Forty-eight development indicators, including the $1 a day poverty rate, are used to measure progress toward the goals. For poverty, the goal was to reduce the extreme poverty rate by half, from nearly 46 percent in 1990 to 23 percent in 2015. With the 2005 rate already at 27 percent, it appeared likely that this goal would be met, but the dramatic worldwide increase in food prices since 2008 (brought about in part by U.S. ethanol subsidies) threatens to undo much of the improvement. Although much of the developing world has made significant progress toward achieving these goals, conditions in sub-Saharan Africa have stagnated or gotten worse on many indicators.

It is generally the position of the World Bank and the International Monetary Fund that free market reforms and reducing political corruption

TABLE 9.1

Millennium Development Goals, Selected Indicators

Developing Nations	1990-91	1999-01	2009	2015 goals
Poverty rate	46	36	27*	23
Undernourishment rate	20	16	16*	10
School enrollment	80	82	89	100
- girls	76	79	88	100
- boys	86	85	90	100
Literacy rate, age 15-24	80	85	88	100
- girls	75	81	85	100
- boys	86	89	91	100
Child mortality rate	99	84	66	33
Marternal mortality rate	4.4	3.7	2.9	1.1
HIV prevalence	.3	.8	.8	**
Sub-Saharan Africa				
Poverty rate	58	58	51*	29
Undernourishment rate	36	30	26*	18
School enrollment	54	58	76	100
- girls	49	54	75	100
- boys	58	62	78	100
Literacy rate, age 15-24	65	69	72	100
- girls	58	62	67	100
- boys	73	76	77	100
Child mortality rate	180	160	129	60
Marternal mortality rate	8.7	7.9	6.4	2.2
HIV prevalence	2.1	5.5	4.7	**

*2005 **reverse the incease

Poverty: % of population below $1.25 a day level

Undernourishment: % below minimum dietary energy consumption

School enollment: primary and secondary enrollments, % of age group

Child death rate: under age 5 deaths per 1,000 live births

Maternal mortality rate: maternal dalth per 1,000 live births

HIV rate: % aged 15 to 49 with HIV

Source: UN, _Millenium Deveopment Goals Report, 2011_

will provide the solutions to poverty in the developing world. African countries generally rank among the world's poorest nations, and their governments typically rank as the most corrupt, as measured by Transparency International's Corruption Perceptions Index.[7]

Poorer nations tend to be more corrupt than wealthy nations (figure 9.2), but whether political corruption is the cause or the effect of poverty is a matter of much dispute. Bob Geldof, activist and organizer of the Live Aid and Live 8 concerts, argues that "Africa is not mired in corruption, it is mired in poverty. Corruption is a by-product of poverty, just like dying of famine or AIDS."[8] The free market policies advocated by the World Bank and the International Monetary Fund (IMF) are also the subject of much controversy. Critics of the World Bank and the IMF argue that the organizations' advocacy of market reforms—such as privatization, reduced government subsidies, free trade, and business deregulation—result in reductions in necessary social services and increased poverty and inequality.

The conservative Heritage Foundation includes the *Corruption Perception Index* as one of ten broad factors that make up its *Economic Freedom Index*. In general, "free" nations have low taxes and small government, are open to foreign trade, respect private property rights, have minimal regulation of banking and finance, and do not burden businesses with excessive government regulation. Although on a worldwide scale, richer nations generally score high on the freedom index (the United States ranked 9th in 2011, with a score of 78 out of 100), the general relationship between economic freedom and economic growth is sometimes at odds with expectations. For sub-Saharan Africa, for example, "less free" nations have actually seen better economic growth than "free" ones (figure 9.3).

On the other hand, the dramatic reductions in East Asian and South Asian poverty since the 1980s (shown in figure 9.1) can be credited to free

Figure 9.2. Corruption and Poverty in African Nations.

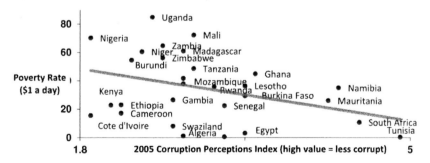

Sources: World Bank, PovcalNet; Transparency International.

Figure 9.3. Real GDP Growth Rate and Economic Freedom, 37 Sub-Saharan Nations.

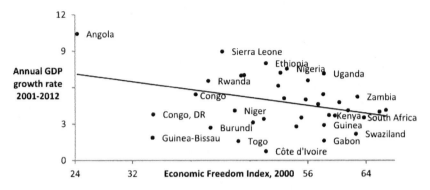

Sources: OECD.StatExtracts, Heritage Foundation.

market reforms in China and India, especially the privatization of agriculture in China and the reduction in restrictions on free trade in both countries.

Issues of Data Reliability

While both the United Nations and the World Bank strive to provide accurate and reliable measures of poverty and other social and economic indicators, much of the poverty data is of uncertain quality. Many of the poorest nations—such as Zimbabwe or the Democratic Republic of the Congo—lack the bureaucratic infrastructure to conduct accurate demographic counts, and those poor nations with large government bureaucracies may produce data designed merely to make the bureaucracies look good.

Constructing the poverty measure involves two steps: (1) determining the distribution of income (or consumption) across a country's households (i.e., how many households live at each income level), and (2) defining what the $1 and $2 a day standard means in local currency. In the case of the World Bank's poverty measure, the base data are derived from national surveys of household consumer expenditure or income conducted at widely varying intervals in each country: approximately every six years in India, annually or biennially in China, rarely or never in many of the poorest nations. Typically, the household consumption survey asks a member of the household to report the household's food consumption and other purchases over the previous week or month. The data are then extrapolated into yearly figures. The base data provide estimates of the percentage of households living at each level of consumption or income. Those percentages are then used to estimate the poverty rate using national standards and to generate measures of economic growth and income distribution (such as the Gini coefficient).[9]

Next, one has to determine what level of national consumer expenditure corresponds to the World Bank's $1 and $2 a day standards. Because a U.S. dollar may not buy the same amount of consumer goods in each country, the income level is adjusted using an estimate of the purchasing power of each country's national currency. The measurement requires additional household surveys to determine what commodities people in the country typically consume and retail business surveys to detail the price of those commodities. The consumer price surveys are similar to those used to estimate consumer inflation in the United States, but whereas the United States conducts the surveys every month and releases the results within a month, the World Bank's estimates take much longer.[10]

Despite the problems with the World Bank measure, it is preferred over the often-cited measure of poverty provided in the CIA's *The World Factbook*,[11] which lists each nation's own measure of its poverty. Because each nation has its own definition of the level of income that denotes poverty, the data are not comparable, and there is little practical use for the data.

MEASURING POVERTY IN WEALTHY NATIONS

When the World Bank estimates the total world population living below the $1 a day level, it makes the reasonable assumption that almost no one in the developed world would fall below the standard. In the United States, a family receiving food stamps would easily exceed the $2 a day consumption standard. Beginning in 1983, the *Luxembourg Income Study* (LIS) began compiling a collection of household income surveys conducted (usually) annually by many of the world's wealthiest countries. The LIS database now includes income surveys from twenty-nine countries. Under the direction of Timothy Smeeding and Lee Rainwater, the LIS center adjusts the national survey data to provide for consistent measures of income distribution and poverty across most OECD nations and several others.

Unlike the World Bank poverty measures, the poverty indicator most commonly reported by the LIS is a relative measure: the percentage of persons living in families earning below 50 percent (or some other percentage) of the national median family income, adjusted for family size (figure 9.4). Unlike the U.S. measure of poverty (described below), the LIS measure is based on disposable income (income after taxes) and includes some "near-cash" income, such as (in the U.S. case) food stamps. Among the OECD nations for

Figure 9.4. Child Poverty Rate: % below the U.S. Poverty Line, 19 OECD Nations, circa 1990.

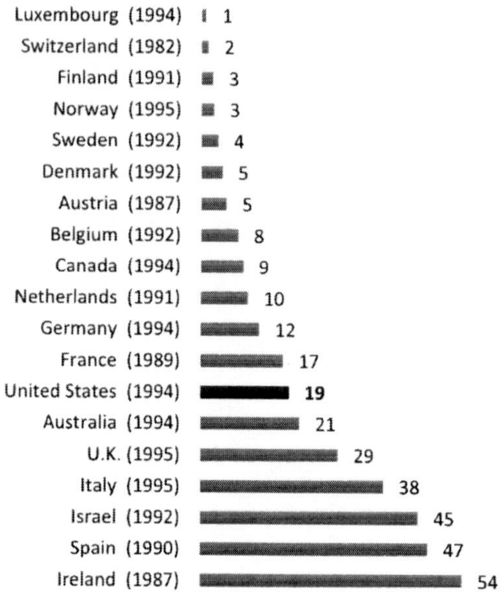

Luxembourg (1994)	1
Switzerland (1982)	2
Finland (1991)	3
Norway (1995)	3
Sweden (1992)	4
Denmark (1992)	5
Austria (1987)	5
Belgium (1992)	8
Canada (1994)	9
Netherlands (1991)	10
Germany (1994)	12
France (1989)	17
United States (1994)	**19**
Australia (1994)	21
U.K. (1995)	29
Italy (1995)	38
Israel (1992)	45
Spain (1990)	47
Ireland (1987)	54

Source: Bradbury and Jäntti, 1999.

which there are data, the U.S ranks 19th out of 21 countries on both overall and child poverty (table 9.2). The Gini coefficient is a broader measure of income distribution. A Gini coefficient of zero indicates an equal distribution of income (every household having the same income), while a score of 1 would indicate that one person has all of the income. On this measure, the United States consistently ranks with the highest level of income inequality among wealthy nations, on par with many of the poorest African nations.[12]

Smeeding and Rainwater have used these data in a series of reports and a book addressing international differences in child poverty, calling attention to the consistently highest rates of child poverty in the United States (table 9.2).[13]

Note, however, that the high rate of child poverty is based on a relative threshold measure of poverty, and the United States has the highest median family income of the nations shown. To correct for this, a 1999 study by Bradbury and Jäntti[14] produced estimates of child poverty using the U.S. poverty-level standard of $15,300 for a family of four, and adjusting for differences in purchasing power. Using this absolute poverty-level standard, the United States ranked thirteenth in child poverty (figure 9.4). For a

TABLE 9.2
Poverty and Inequality, 21 OECD Nations

	Relative Poverty Rate*		Gini
	All Persons	Children	Coefficient
Denmark, 2004	5.6	3.9	.228
Sweden, 2005	5.6	4.7	.237
Finland, 2004	6.5	3.7	.252
Norway, 2004	7.1	4.9	.256
Austria, 2004	7.1	7.0	.269
Hungary, 2005	7.4	9.9	.289
Switzerland, 2004	8.0	9.2	.268
Germany, 2004	8.5	10.7	.278
Luxembourg, 2004	8.8	13.3	.268
Poland, 2004	11.5	17.2	.320
U.K., 2004	11.6	14.0	.345
Italy, 2004	12.1	18.4	.338
Australia, 2003	12.2	14.0	.312
Greece, 2004	12.5	13.2	.329
Canada, 2004	13.0	16.8	.318
Korea, 2006	14.0	10.4	.311
Spain, 2004	14.1	17.2	.315
Ireland, 2000	16.2	15.8	.313
United States, 2004	**17.3**	**21.2**	**.372**
Mexico, 2004	18.4	22.2	.458
Israel, 2005	19.2	25.3	.370

*persons in families below 50% of median income
Source: Luxembourg Income Study

country that has always thought of itself as a middle-class society, the high level of both absolute and relative poverty in the United States is a disturbing economic phenomenon.

MEASURING POVERTY IN THE UNITED STATES

In 1963, Mollie Orshansky, an economist at the Social Security Administration, undertook the task of determining just how many people in the United States were poor.[15] Although conservative and liberal scholars have debated the merits of the indicator ever since, the U.S. poverty rate statistic that she developed remains today as one of the most commonly used measures of the nation's economic health.

To measure the poverty rate, it was first necessary to determine the threshold for classifying families as poor. Orshansky began with studies of food budgets conducted by the Department of Agriculture in the mid-1950s. The U.S. Department of Agriculture had developed an Economy Food Plan, a budget designed to meet the basic nutritional needs of families. For 1963, the Economy Food Plan cost a family of four (two adults and two children) an average of $1,033 per year. A separate 1955 study of family budgets had determined that American families (all families) spent an average of one-third of their budget on food. Multiplying the food budget by three, Orshansky set $3,100 as the poverty threshold for a family of four.

The threshold is adjusted for family size and for changes in the *Consumer Price Index* (note: not for changes in cost of the food budget). For 2010, the resulting poverty threshold for a family of four stood at $22,113. Persons living in four-person families where the total family income was less than $22,113 were classified as poor, and those with higher incomes are classified as not poor. Over 46 million Americans were living in poor families (15.1 percent of the total population) and 9.2 million families were poor (11.7 percent of the families).

The U.S. poverty rate fell sharply in the 1960s, reaching its lowest point in 1973, and has fluctuated in a narrow range since then (figure 9.5). Poverty trends generally reflect changes in the economy: the declines in the 1990s reflect the economic prosperity of the Clinton administration years, and the increases before and after those years reflect the economic downturns of the two Bush administrations. The last three years of the data series recorded the largest increases in the history of the poverty measurement. When the 2011 data are released in the fall of 2012, the poverty rate will probably reach a new forty-year high.

The Bureau of Labor Statistics and the Census Bureau derive income and poverty estimates from the annual Current Population Survey (CPS), based on a national sample of approximately 100,000 families. For the U.S. population as a whole, the sampling error (based on a 90 percent confidence interval)

Figure 9.5. U.S. Poverty Rates for Persons and Families, 1959–2010.

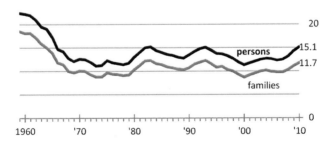

Source: Census Bureau, Historical Poverty Tables.

is approximately plus or minus .2 percent. Thus, if the reported poverty rate is 15 percent, we can be 90 percent sure that the true rate is between 14.8 and 15.2 percent. For subpopulations in the survey (e.g., children, or two-parent households) the sampling errors are greater, depending on the sample size.

Since 2000, the Census Bureau has provided additional poverty estimates based on its continuous year-round American Community Survey. In 2006, this survey had a sample size of three million addresses, providing reliable poverty estimates for all states and areas with a population greater than 65,000.

Because the CPS survey includes many demographic questions about age, family structure and marital status, race, and ethnicity, the data allow for very detailed analyses of the demographics of poverty (figure 9.6). A substantial portion of the black–white poverty gap, but not the white–Hispanic gap, can be accounted for by the high proportion of black families headed by single mothers (table 9.3).

Senator Daniel Moynihan (D-NY) often called attention to the disparity in trends in poverty rates for children and the elderly.[16] In the 1960s, poverty rates fell for both groups, but after the early 1970s, the child poverty rate began to increase while the elderly poverty rate continued to decline— to the point where the elderly are now much less likely to be poor than the population as a whole (figure 9.7). These trends, Moynihan argued, were the result of the substantial increases in Social Security and Supplemental Security Income benefits for the elderly after 1970 and the steady decline in funding for Aid to Families with Dependent Children and other programs that targeted benefits to families with children. By implication, the failure of Congress to enact the welfare reform plan that Moynihan authored for the Nixon administration in 1969 was largely to blame.

Figure 9.6. Poverty Rates by Family Status and Race and Ethnicity, 2010.

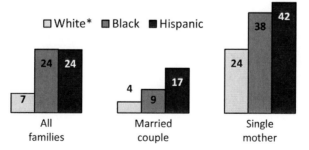

* White alone, non-Hispanic.

Source: Census Bureau, Historical Poverty Tables.

TABLE 9.3
Family Status and Poverty Rates by Race and Ethnicity, 2010

	Family Status			Poverty Rate	
	% Married couple	% Single father	% Single mother	Actual	Adjusted for family status*
White	81	6	13	7	7
Black	45	10	46	24	14
Hispanic	63	11	26	24	21
All Families	74	7	19	12	10

*assuming 81% married couple, 6% single-father, 13% single mother
Source: Census Bureau, Historical Poverty Tables

In 2011, the Census Bureau issued a revised supplemental poverty measure that took into account geographical differences in housing costs and included many of the income-related resources (such as food stamps and the Earned Income Tax Credit [EITC]) and medical and child care costs that the traditional measure missed. Under the new measure, the overall poverty rate was only slightly higher (15.2 percent versus 15.1 percent), but there were significant differences in the child and elderly poverty rates. For children, the new estimate was lower, at 18.2 percent compared to 22.5 percent under the official measure. For the elderly, the rate was almost 7 percentage points higher (15.9 percent versus 9 percent).

Problems with the U.S. Poverty Measure

There have been many complaints that the poverty statistics either overestimate or underestimate the true poverty rate. Liberals say that poverty is higher than the numbers indicate, while conservatives insist that the

Figure 9.7. U.S. Poverty Rates, by Age, 1959–2010.

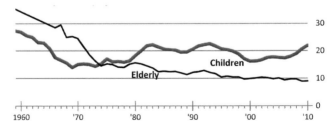

Source: Census Bureau, Historical Poverty Tables.

numbers exaggerate the poverty rate—although these claims are made more or less strenuously depending on which party is in power.

Liberals often complain that the poverty thresholds are too low. Although food was one-third of a family budget in the 1950s, it is one-seventh now. Considering this, they insist, would call for a higher threshold.[17] In addition, poverty thresholds are adjusted for price inflation, rather than for income. Because incomes generally rise faster than prices, the poverty thresholds are much lower today compared to the average family income than they were in the 1960s. Additionally, the poverty measures do not fully capture what we mean by poverty. Families with incomes above the poverty line may nevertheless be deeply in debt, often because of large medical bills.

Conservatives argue that the thresholds are set too high in part because the Consumer Price Index used to adjust the poverty threshold has been shown to exaggerate the level of inflation as much as 1 percentage point per year. They also note that the definition of "money income" used in the measure does not include noncash income such as food stamp benefits, public housing, or Medicaid benefits. Because the income measure is based on pretax income, it does not take into account the EITC benefits that many working families with children receive.

Although there is some basis for both claims, one has to understand that poverty is an inherently subjective concept to begin with: There is no such thing as a true poverty rate. Most of the complaints about the poverty rate statistic concern its validity (whether the statistic measures what it is supposed to measure), but questions about the statistic's reliability (the consistency of the measurement) are often more to the point.

Consider the conclusion that might be drawn from the trends in child and elderly poverty rates in figure 9.7. Because families with children are much more likely to receive EITC and food stamp benefits, which are not counted as income, than are the elderly, the disparity is not as great as the data indicate. Also, because the EITC benefits were first offered in the 1980s and substantially increased in the first year of the Clinton administration, real child poverty has declined at a faster rate than the data show. On the other hand, because many of the elderly poor have savings and assets that do not enter into the calculation of their family income, the poverty rate statistic may overestimate their level of poverty as well.

Measuring Income Inequality

The income data used to derive the poverty measurements can also be used to address many other issues related to income inequality. Thus, figure 9.8 shows trends in the share of aggregate family income for the richest

Figure 9.8. Share of Aggregate Family Income, 1947–2010.

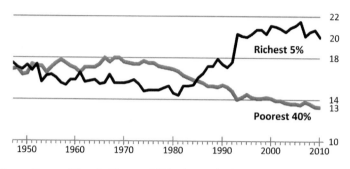

Source: Census Bureau, Historical Income Tables (Inequality).

5 percent of households and the poorest 40 percent. Since 1980, the wealthy have seen their share of family income steadily increase.

Note, however, that conservatives sometimes object that the income distribution data reflect changes in household composition: The highest income groups tend to comprise larger households than the lower income groupings. The top household income quintile (containing the wealthiest 20 percent of the nation's households), for example, contained one quarter of the population in 2005, the bottom quintile, less than 15 percent.[18]

Spinning the Income and Poverty Statistics

In addition to the poverty measures, the Census Bureau's *Current Population Survey* provides several different indicators of income and earnings. The choice of indicators and the indicators' base (whether persons, families, or households) can lead to different conclusions, and comparisons of the different measures can lead to even more insightful conclusions, but readers should be aware that the choices provide many opportunities to cherry pick the data.[19] Next we will examine two arguments using the poverty and income data, one liberal and one conservative, to demonstrate how data selection can shape the authors' conclusions.

On the liberal side, we will consider just a piece of a larger argument made by *New York Times* columnist Paul Krugman in his 2007 book *The Conscience of a Liberal*. Krugman's main argument is that conservative tax and social policies since the Reagan administration have produced a level of social and economic inequality in America little different from that of the pre–Depression era Gilded Age. Much of his argument is based on evidence, such as that presented in figure 9.8, of rising income inequality since the early 1980s.

A small part of Krugman's argument is a claim that the typical American family has made little if any economic progress over these years.[20] In presenting his evidence, Krugman employs several different income measures and takes great care to present his numerical evidence in terms general readers can understand. He begins by conceding that America is indeed a wealthier nation: "Average income—the total income of the nation, divided by the number of people—has gone up substantially since 1973, the last year of the great boom."[21]

Krugman does not cite the actual data, but he is correct: Between 1973 and 2005 (the last year of the data cited in his book), per capita income in constant dollars increased 54 percent (row A in table 9.4). The average, or mean, household income has not increased quite as fast, only 37 percent, because households have become smaller and there are more households per person (row B).

Krugman attributes the increase to the growth in productivity spurred largely by the technological advances of the era. He notes, however, that the average income is not a valid measure of how well most people are doing. "If Bill Gates walks into a bar," he explains, "the average wealth of the bar's clientele soars, but the men already there when he walked in are no wealthier than before." The better indicator, he writes, would be the median income (half the incomes are above and half are below the median). When Gates walks into a bar, the median income hardly changes at all.[22]

TABLE 9.4
Measures of Income Change, 1973-2005*

	1973	2005	% change	trend
A. Per capita income	$16,263	$25,036	+54	..--......ıllıllıllllll
B. Mean household income	46,268	63,344	+37	........ıllıllllllll
C. Median household income	40,008	46,326	+16	....ıllllıı
D. Median earnings, men**	42,573	41,386	-3	.........----.....---....
Median personal income:**				
E. men, ages 35-44	45,785	40,964	-11	....----....-----ıllllıllllll
F. women ages, 35-44	15,642	25,435	+63	.. ...---...ıllıllllllll

*in constant 2005 dollars
** full-time year-round workers
Source: U.S. Census Bureau, Historical Income Tables

Here, Krugman finds that "median household income adjusted for inflation, grew modestly from 1973 to 2005. . . . The total gain was about 16 percent" (row C). Krugman evaluates this evidence and concedes (commendably) that in some respects the 16 percent increase may understate the true increase in prosperity, as inflation adjustments may overstate the true inflation rate and do not capture the improvements in the quality of products that today's dollar can buy. On the other hand, he notes that the household income growth has been achieved mostly by more Americans working and working longer hours. The increase in women entering the workforce has been a good thing, Krugman says, "but a gain in family income that occurs because a spouse goes to work is not the same thing as a wage increase." He points out that the earnings of men working year-round full-time have actually declined since 1973 (the 3 percent decline in row D) and that when we compare men of the same age, the decline is even greater: "If we look at the earnings of men aged thirty-five to forty-four—men who would a generation ago often support stay-at-home wives—we find that the inflation-adjusted wages were 12 percent *higher* in 1973 than they are now" (row E).[23]

From this, Krugman concludes that "the typical American family hasn't made clear progress in the last thirtysomething years."[24] This conclusion rests on a careful but one-sided presentation of the evidence. It is true that the typical family has not made clear progress, but only if you mean the typical 1973 family. In 1973, there were 3.4 persons in the United States for every family; by 2005 that had declined to 3.1.[25] The men with stay-at-home wives who supported a family in 1973 are supporting smaller families today, often with two incomes. Moreover, women's earnings have risen substantially over the same period, something Krugman doesn't mention. Women aged 35 to 44 have seen their inflation-adjusted income increase 63 percent (row F).

Krugman precisely defines his indicators using the exact Census Bureau terminology, allowing this reader to verify the accuracy of the statistics (and, thus, to construct table 9.4). He makes critical distinctions in interpreting alternative measures of income and acknowledges the limitations of at least some of his data, but he leaves out some critical evidence that does not fit his conclusion.

As one-sided as Krugman's presentation of the evidence is, it is the very model of a fair and balanced presentation when considered alongside the following statistical argument from the other side of the political spectrum.

It took place in an exchange between talk show host Bill O'Reilly and "Larry," one of his radio show callers:

CALLER: Hi, Bill.
O'REILLY: Larry.

CALLER: Let's see, poverty is up since Bush took office.

O'REILLY: That's not true.

CALLER: It is true.

O'REILLY: I have the stats right here, Larry.

CALLER: I just looked at the figures. Gun crime is up since George Bush took office.

O'REILLY: All right, Larry, hold it, hold it, hold it. Let's deal with one at a time. The only fair comparison is halfway through Clinton's term, halfway through Bush's term, Okay? That's the only fair comparison. You gotta go real time.

CALLER: Bill, I —

O'REILLY: Poverty is down, Larry, one full percent in real time from 1996, halfway through Clinton 2004, halfway through Bush. That is the truth, Larry, and if you're not willing to acknowledge that's the truth, this conversation is over.[26]

O'Reilly's claim, which I heard repeated on two "no-spin zone" Fox News cable TV broadcasts, is based on two entirely accurate statistics combined with a lot of very faulty reasoning. O'Reilly's statistics are accurate: Bush's fourth-year poverty rate was a full percent lower than Clinton's fourth-year poverty rate (figure 9.9). And O'Reilly's interpretation of the two numbers involves what seems like a reasonable premise: It would be unfair to compare what President Bush achieved in four years with what President Clinton achieved over eight years. Nevertheless, O'Reilly is unwilling to acknowledge that Larry is also telling the truth and providing a better interpretation of the statistics. Where O'Reilly goes wrong is in using the rate at the end of the first term rather than the change in the rate over the presidents' four years in office: The poverty rate went down

Figure 9.9. Poverty Rates for Persons, 1988–2004.

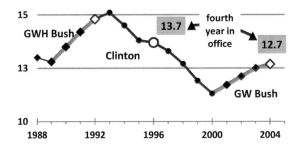

Source: Census Bureau, Historic Poverty Tables.

1.2 percentage points in Clinton's first term and up 1.4 percentage points in Bush's first term. And it fell another 2.4 points in Clinton's second term. Viewed another way, O'Reilly gives Bush all the credit for the decline in the poverty rate since the midpoint of Clinton's term in office, but all of that decline, and more, took place while Clinton was in office.

I was again watching *The O'Reilly Factor* six years later when he happened upon another poverty statistic:

> O'REILLY: First some stats. There are about 46 million Americans living below the poverty line, 15 percent of the population. . . . But here's the stat that may provide some perspective on poverty.
>
> According to the Department of Health and Human Services, about nine percent of Americans have some kind of substance dependence. Most of those people cannot earn a living. So let's do the math: 15 percent poor, nine percent addicted. Maybe poverty is not exclusively an economic problem.[27]

Again, O'Reilly cites two statistics accurately and connects them with what might seem to be a reasonable premise: "Most of those people cannot earn a living." Reasonable, that is, until you start thinking about all the famous rock stars and celebrities with substance abuse problems. It is probable that his "nine percent addicted" stat comes from the 2003 National Survey on Drug Use and Health that found 9.1 percent of the population over age 12 were classified with "substance dependence or abuse." The same study found that over 10 percent of adults who were employed full-time were classified with substance dependence, and that 77 percent of the "addicted" were actually employed. Only 5.5 million adults were unemployed and classified with substance dependence or abuse.[28] Using the same kind of bogus math that O'Reilly does, we could say: "46 million Americans are poor, 5 million are addicted."[29]

I don't know what conclusion O'Reilly would have drawn had he cited another "stat" from the same report: 9.1 percent of American adults suffer from serious mental illness, identical to the percentage "addicted."

It is not true that "you can prove anything you want with statistics." It is true that you can find and/or present statistics in support of just about any claim, but it takes more than just statistics to reach any conclusion. To "prove" something with statistics usually takes at least two things: the statistics and some thinking. When people make bogus claims about numbers, it is usually the thinking, not the statistics, that is at fault.

NOTES

1. Michel Chossudovsky, "Global Falsehoods: How the World Bank and the UNDP Distort the Figures on Global Poverty," Transnational Foundation for Peace and Future Research, 1999, at http://www.transnational.org/SAJT/features/chossu_worldbank.html; Garth L. Mangum, Stephen L. Mangum, and Andrew M. Summ, *The Persistence of Poverty in the United States* (Baltimore: Johns Hopkins University Press, 2003).

2. Robert Rector and Rea Hederman Jr., "Two Americas: One Rich, One Poor? Understanding Income Inequality in the United States," Heritage Foundation Backgrounder 1791, August 24, 2004, at http://www.heritage.org/Research/Taxes/bg1791.cfm.

3. In order to make the standards close to the national poverty standards of a set of nations, the actual standards are $1.08 and $2.15 a day.

4. Shaohua Chen and Martin Ravallion, "How Have the World's Poorest Fared since the Early 1980s?" Policy Research Working Paper 3341, World Bank, 2000, at http://ideas.repec.org/p/wbk/wbrwps/3341.html.

5. World Bank, *World Development Report 2007: Development and the Next Generation* (Washington, DC: World Bank, 2006).

6. United Nations Development Programme, *Human Development Report 2006: Beyond Scarcity: Power, Poverty and the Global Water Crisis* (New York: UNDP, 2006), at http://hdr.undp.org/hdr2006.

7. Transparency International, *Global Corruption Report 2007* (Cambridge, UK: Cambridge University Press, 2007).

8. BBC News, "G8 Leaders 'Real Stars of Show,'" July 2, 2005, at http://news.bbc.co.uk/2/hi/uk_news/4643451.stm.

9. Shaohua Chen and Martin Ravallion, "The Developing World Is Poorer Than We Thought, but No Less Successful in the Fight against Poverty," *Quarterly Journal of Economics* 125(4): 1577–1625.

10. Sanjay G. Reddy and Thomas W. Pogge, "How Not to Count the Poor," Version 6.2, 2005, at http://www.columbia.edu/~sr793/count.pdf.

11. U.S. Central Intelligence Agency, *The World Factbook*, at http://www.cia.gov/library/publications/the-world-factbook/index.html.

12. Timothy M. Smeeding, "Public Policy, Economic Inequality, and Poverty: The United States in Comparative Perspective," *Social Science Quarterly* 86(s1): 955–83.

13. Lee Rainwater and Timothy M. Smeeding, *Poor Kids in a Rich Country: America's Children in Comparative Perspective* (New York: Russell Sage Foundation, 2003).

14. Bruce Bradbury and Markus Jäntti, "Child Poverty across Industrialized Nations," September 1999, at http://www.unicef-irc.org/publications/pdf/eps71.pdf.

15. Gordon M. Fisher, "Remembering Mollie Orshansky—The Developer of the Poverty Thresholds," *Social Security Bulletin*, 68, no. 3 (2008).

16. Daniel Patrick Moynihan, *Family and Nation* (New York: Harcourt Brace Jovanovich, 1987).

17. Garth L. Mangum, Stephen L. Mangum, and Andrew M. Sum, *The Persistence of Poverty in the United States* (Baltimore: Johns Hopkins University Press, 2003), 81. The

argument does not take into account that the threshold has been adjusted upward for inflation in all consumer goods, not just for increases in food prices.

18. Rector and Hederman, "Two Americas: One Rich, One Poor?"

19. A household consists of a person or group sharing the same housing unit. A family, or more precisely a family household, consists of two or more related persons in the same housing unit.

20. Paul Krugman, *The Conscience of a Liberal* (New York: Norton, 2007), 124–28.

21. Krugman, *The Conscience of a Liberal*, 125.

22. Krugman, *The Conscience of a Liberal*, 125.

23. Note that Krugman says 1973 wages were 12% higher than 2005 wages, but table 6.3 shows an 11% decline in income from 1973 to 2005. Both numbers are correct: Krugman is using the 2005 data as his divisor. I am assuming "wages" refers to the median income measure, as this is most consistent with the numbers he reports. Krugman, *The Conscience of a Liberal*, 127.

24. Krugman, *The Conscience of a Liberal*, 128.

25. U.S. Census Bureau, Historical Poverty Tables, table 2 (people) and table 4 (families), at http://www.census.gov/hhes/www/poverty/data/historical/.

26. Media Matters for America, "O'Reilly Defended False Clinton–Bush Poverty Comparison as 'the Only Accurate Measuring Stick,'" September 16, 2005, at mediamatters .org/items/200509160002.

27. "Fierce Debate Erupts between O'Reilly, Cornel West, and Tavis Smiley," at http://nation.foxnews.com/herman-cain/2011/10/11/hot-debate-oreilly-vs -tavis-smiley-and-cornel-west.

28. Substance Abuse and Mental Health Services Administration, *Results from the 2003 National Survey on Drug Use and Health: National Finding*, Office of Applied Studies, 2004 NSDUH Series H-25, DHHS Publication No. SMA 04-3964. (Rockville, MD: Department of Health and Human Services, 2004).

29. This is bogus for many reasons: A third of poor adults are actually employed, there were only 35 million poor in 2003 when the study was done, only 20 million of them were adults, and many unemployed persons live in non-poor households.

Index

About the Author

Gary M. Klass is associate professor in the Department of Politics and Government, Illinois State University.